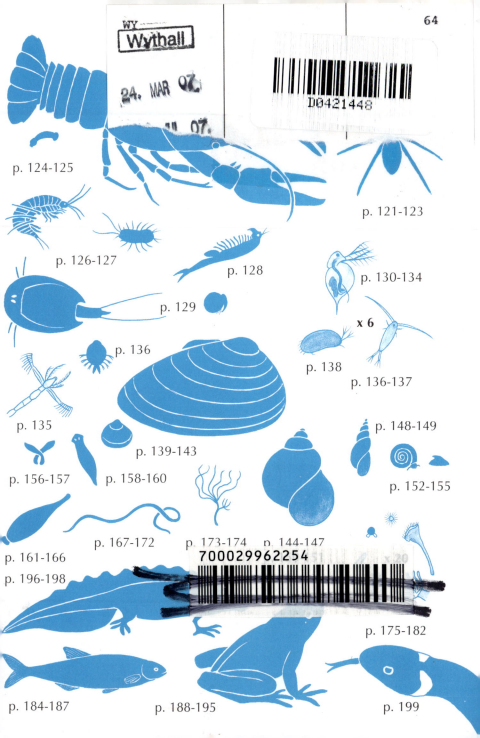

p. 124-125

p. 121-123

p. 126-127

p. 128

p. 130-134

p. 129

x 6

p. 136

p. 138

p. 136-137

p. 135

p. 148-149

p. 139-143

p. 156-157

p. 158-160

p. 152-155

p. 167-172

p. 173-174

p. 144-147

p. 161-166

p. 196-198

p. 175-182

p. 184-187

p. 188-195

p. 199

Anatomy

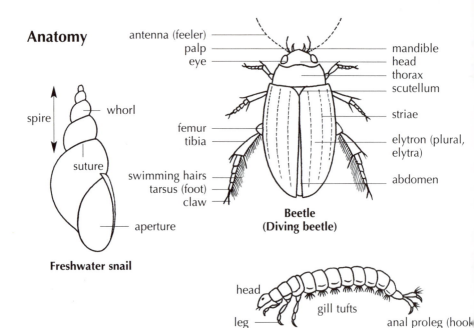

Freshwater snail

- spire
- whorl
- suture
- aperture

Beetle (Diving beetle)

- antenna (feeler)
- palp
- eye
- femur
- tibia
- swimming hairs
- tarsus (foot)
- claw
- mandible
- head
- thorax
- scutellum
- striae
- elytron (plural, elytra)
- abdomen

- head
- leg
- gill tufts
- anal proleg (hook)

Larva (caddis fly)

Complete metamorphosis

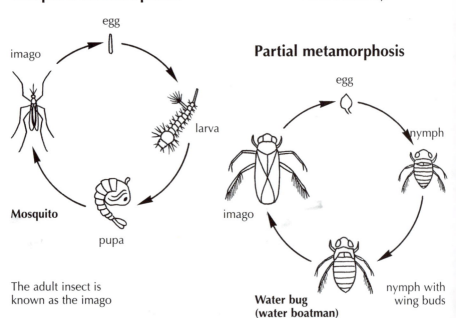

- egg
- imago
- larva
- pupa

Mosquito

The adult insect is known as the imago

Partial metamorphosis

- egg
- nymph
- nymph with wing buds
- imago

Water bug (water boatman)

Small freshwater creatures

LARS-HENRIK OLSEN
JAKOB SUNESEN
BENTE VITA PEDERSEN

Translated by Network Communications
and edited by Martin Walters

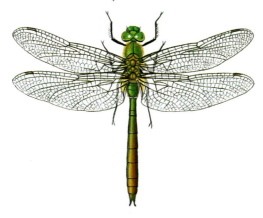

OXFORD
UNIVERSITY PRESS

y of Oxford.
earch, scholar-
, New York,
:utta, Cape
<ong, Istanbul,
·y, Mumbai,
nto, Warsaw,

ress

Published in the United States
by Oxford University Press, Inc., New York

English edition © Oxford University Press 2001

Små dyr i sø og å was first published by G.E.C. Gad Publishers in
1999

© Gyldendalske Boghandel, Nordisk Forlag A/S

Database right Oxford University Press (maker)

First published 2001

British Library Cataloguing in Publication Data
Data available

Library of Congress Cataloging in Publication Data
Data available

ISBN-13 : 978-0-19-850798-7
ISBN-10 : 0-19-850798-4

Typeset by Narayana Press
Printed in Hongkong

Contents

Introduction

Freshwater contains a fascinating and remarkably varied array of small animals, and just a peep down into the water will reveal some of these. Most are active during the day, making them relatively easy to catch and study. There are, however, many types of freshwater, and the wildlife in it will not be the same everywhere – each species has its preferred environment, and its own way of life.

The best equipment for catching small animals is a sieve on a pole, or a net. Most water animals die quickly in the air, so take a plastic box or a glass jar with you, together with forceps and a magnifying glass for studying the animals close up.

Use the inside front cover of the book to look up references to adult animals. The back of the book shows silhouettes of nymphs and larvae.

Most animals are shown larger than life; unless stated otherwise, the degree of enlargement is given at the top of every page. The animals have been painted from life as far as possible. All known animals and plants have an internationally recognised scientific name. This is a binomial, consisting of a generic name, followed by a species epithet. For example, the Water Spider is called *Argyroneta aquatica*. The term sp. (species) after a genus name, e.g. *Tabanus* sp., means an undefined species of the genus *Tabanus*, i.e. a kind of horse-fly.

In practice it is often only possible to determine the genus of an animal, as the more precise identification as to species may require study under the microscope.

Body lengths stated in the descriptions refer to the length from the front edge of the head to the end of the abdomen. Wingspan is the distance between the wingtips when the wings are extended.

Towards the end of the book there are descriptions of special environments with their typical fauna.

Take care of animals and treat them as well as you can. Remember to put them back where you caught them.

Have fun!

Lars-Henrik Olsen

Owlet moths

These moths are active primarily at night. They are powerfully built, with dark, camouflage-coloured forewings, often with distinct colours on the hind wings. The forewings usually have three distinct spots: a ring-shaped spot near the wing's centre, a kidney-shaped mark further down, and an elongated spot beyond the ring-mark, near the wing's rear edge. The wings are held roofwise or flat over each other at rest. Owlet moths are often attracted to light. Most overwinter as eggs. The larvae are normally short, fat and slightly hairy, and have three pairs of legs and five pairs of prolegs.

Bulrush Wainscot
Nonagria typhae

Wingspan 42-52 mm. Forewings are brown, with light and dark spots and often with a light, arched border along the edge and around dark spots. Light grey or yellowish hind wings. Occasionally found far from water. Common; flies August-October. Larva, up to 50 mm, is light brown or whitish-yellow, lightly flesh-coloured, and found in stems of bulrush and club-rushes, May-June. The grown larva mines a broad tunnel in the lower part of the stems, where it pupates.

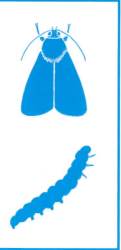

larva   bulrush

Large Wainscot
Rhizedra lutosa

Wingspan 37-56 mm. Forewings light brown, reddish
or ivory. Hind wings white. Forewings and hind
wings have a row of small black spots. Common near
reedy marshes; often flies in large numbers, September-October. Larva, up to 53 mm, has brown-red
upperside and yellowish underside. Found in root-
stock of reeds, in both fresh and salt water, April-July;
pupates among roots. The reed leaves wither, and the
stems turn yellow.

larva

Twin-spotted Wainscot
Archanara geminipunctata

Wingspan 27-35 mm. Forewing more or less red-
brown with one to two small white spots or dots.
Hind wing is lighter or darker brown-grey. Flies
August-September. Overwinters as egg. Larva found
in reeds from May to July, first in upper part of stem,
then in lower part. Pupates in the litter. In Britain
mainly southern.

larva

Fen Wainscot
Arenostola phragmitidis

Wingspan 28-36 mm. Forewing reddish or yellowish-
grey, with no markings. Hind wings are light or dark
grey. Common near reeds, particularly along shore-
lines, and often in large numbers, July-August.
Larva, up to 18 mm, is light brown with dark spots
and transverse bands. Found in reed straw with dried-
out tips, May-June, and pupates among damp moss
and withered plant matter. In Britain mainly southern.

larva

China-mark moths

China-mark moths are quite large micro-moths, 16-31 mm in length. They have broad forewings and large, often beautifully-patterned hind wings, held down flat at rest. There are often major differences between male and female. They fly through most of the summer and are often seen swarming over water, particularly at twilight, and are attracted to light at night. The larvae feed on water plants and construct cases with them. They overwinter. The pupae are found in cocoons, fastened to water plants beneath the surface.

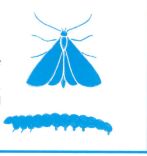

Beautiful China-mark Moth
Nymphula stagnata

Wingspan 16-25 mm. Forewings and hind wings white with dark markings. The central line on the hind wing is only partially double. Flies June-August. Larva, up to 20 mm, mines tunnels in leaves of bur reed and yellow water-lily, boring into the stem, where it overwinters. Those that live under water-lily leaves make a sac from a few pieces of leaf. Pupates under a piece of leaf. Larvae on bur reeds continue to mine the leaves. Common in ponds, lakes and slow-flowing rivers.

right: larva
below: pupa under water-lily leaf, with and without a 'lid'

China-mark moth larvae are easily confused with caddis fly larvae, but they have short legs on the thorax and five pairs of prolegs under the abdomen, while caddis fly larvae have long legs and no prolegs. Adult china-mark moths have scaly wings, while adult caddis flies have hairy wings and very long antennae.

Nymphula nymphaeata

Wingspan 22-33 mm. Female larger than male. Wings are white with dark-brown markings. The central line on the hind wing is clearly double. Flies June-August. Larva, up to 20 mm, makes a flat sac out of two plant pieces on the underside of water-lily leaves, pondweed, frog-bit, bur reed or duckweed. First it mines tunnels around the central vein, but later forms large discoloured areas on the leaves and oval gnawings at the leaf-edges, September-October. Very common in ponds and lakes.

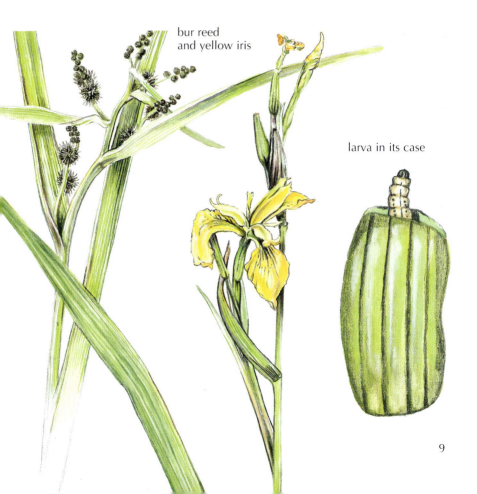

bur reed
and yellow iris

larva in its case

9

♂   ♀

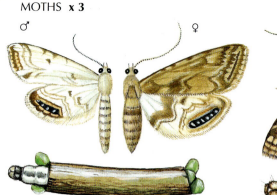

larva in its case

Cataclysta lemnata

Wingspan of female 19-25 mm, male 15-18 mm. Female has light-brown forewings and light hind wings. Male has white wings with dark markings. Easily recognisable by a black patch with blue spots on the hind wings. Flies May-August. Larva, up to 15 mm, makes a long oval tube of small pieces of leaves. Common in ponds and lakes and mainly found under duckweed.

larva

Ringed China-mark Moth
Paraponyx stratiota

Wingspan of female 23-30 mm, male 21-26 mm. Female's forewing is browner in colour than the male's. Flies June-September. Larva, up to 25 mm, covered with tracheal gills, lives in irregular cases made of leaf pieces; found primarily on pondweed. Cuts round sections out of leaves. September-June. In Britain mainly southern.

wingless ♀

♂

larva in case

Field-caddis Water-veneer
Acentria ephemerella

Female is either wingless or has a wingspan of 13-17 mm. Male's wingspan 10-12 mm. Easily recognised by its small size, dark body, and its semi-transparent, whitish wings without spots. Winged females fly long distances. Wingless females, with long hairs on their two rear pairs of legs, swim on the water surface. The male flies in circles close above the water. Mating takes place on the surface, often far from land. Adults live two days at most. Flies at end of June and July-September. Larva, up to 10 mm, found on pondweeds, hornwort etc., eats plant top and spins leaves loosely around itself. Occasionally makes a case of large leaf pieces, sometimes boring into a stem. Found locally in large lakes and in brackish water, particularly in May-June.

CADDIS FLIES

Caddis flies have two pairs of large, often quite broad wings, held roofwise over the body at rest. They have long filamentous antennae, long thin legs with large spurs, and bodies and wings closely covered in hair. They are mostly seen near water at dusk, and can form swarms. They can resemble small moths, but have hairy wings and no proboscis. They eat little, but lap water or nectar from open flowers. Adult caddis flies live only briefly, and are attracted to light, often far from water.

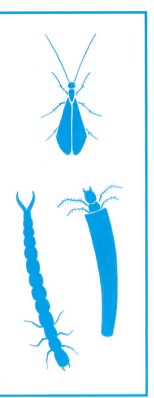

The larvae have a long abdomen and three pairs of legs. They pass through five larval stages and one pupal stage. The head and usually part of the thorax has a hardened surface. Respiration is cutaneous, many having rows of gill threads on the abdomen. The abdominal tip has a pair of terminal hooks, each with a claw. They have silk glands, and most protect their soft abdomens with a transportable web case, which they cover with sand, small stones, plant matter, snail shells, etc. A few species live in the open without a case, and others spin a net on plants or stones, with a case attached to it by spun threads for living in. Those living in the open are predators. Most case-builders feed on plants, algae, detritus etc. The net-spinners are primarily found in running water, feeding on plankton and other organic material they catch in the net.

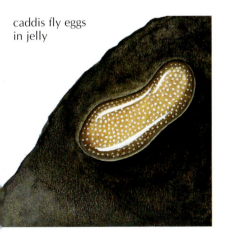

caddis fly eggs
in jelly

Many species mate in flight, casting their egg masses out over the water. The eggs are surrounded by jelly, which swells in water. Some lay eggs on leaves over water, and the young larvae drop down into it in damp weather. Others stick their abdomen in the water and lay their egg masses on water plants or stones. A few creep right down under the surface, enclosed in a thin layer of air, and lay eggs on stones, wood or plants. The eggs of these species have no jelly layer.

larva

Rhyacophila sp.

Wingspan 23-30 mm. Broad, yellowish wings. Antennae approx. same length as body. Flies May-October.

Larva, up to 24 mm long and 3.5 mm across, has silver-white bushy tracheal gills at sides of thorax and abdomen. No larval case. Abdomen is green and head points forward. Short, powerful legs and terminal hooks with large claws allow it to cling tight to irregularities on rocks. It draws a safety thread along behind it, crawls like an inchworm and feeds primarily on other caddis fly larvae and pupae. Builds a hard, elongated, dome-shaped pupal case up to 20 mm in size, of small coarse stones, on the underside of large stones. Pupal sac is red-brown, elongated, cigar-shaped. Found in clean running water with a stony bottom.

Many common species.

pupae with and without case

Agapetus sp.

larval case
from the side,
from above
and from
below

Agapetus sp.

Wingspan 8-10 mm. Narrow wings.
Grey-black forewings with long golden
hair, particularly along the edge. Hind
wings are lighter and iridescent. Male
has a long yellow spine under its abdomen. Occurs locally.
Larva approx. 7 mm long and 1.5 mm
across. Greenish with dark brown head
and thorax, and with small, hard, dark
brown plates on the two back thoracic
segments. Head points forward. Abdomen is thickest in the middle and
has no gills. Terminal hooks are large,
with powerful spines. Builds a bean-
shaped case, up to 8 mm long and 5
mm across, of coarse sand. Underside
is flat, with two tubular openings, surrounded by fine sand. The case cannot
be extended, so the larva must build a
new one or find a larger one after each
of its six moults. Occurs in springs and
fast-flowing streams with stony bottoms.

Agraylea sp.

Wingspan 7.5-9 mm. Long, narrow,
pointed wings have long hair. Forewings often dark with many golden
spots. Short, powerful antennae.
Resembles a small grey moth. It dives
down between filamentous algae to lay
eggs. Flies June-July.
Larva is up to 5 mm long and 1.4 mm
across. Green with yellowish or brown
head and thorax. Head points forward.
Well-developed legs; two rear pairs
very long. Abdomen, without gills, is at
first slender with long thin hairs. It lives
in the open throughout its first four stages, but then the abdomen fattens, and
the larva spins a case up to 8 mm long
and 2.2 mm across using its own silk
and algal filaments. It is compressed,
resembling a spectacle case, and
stands on its edge. The pupal case is
attached to plants by spun thread at all
four corners. Common in the bottom
vegetation and on stones in nutrient-
rich lakes with filamentous algae.
Overwinters as larva.

larva in
case

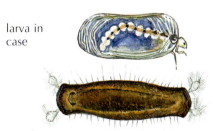

pupal case

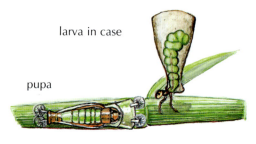

larva in case

pupa

larva in case

Orthotrichia sp.

Larva up to 3 mm. Green with brown head and thorax. Head points forward. Rather delicate legs. Abdomen is compressed, swollen and fattest in the middle, with no gills. Lives in the open for the first four stages, but then spins an oval case like a shark's egg, with openings at either end. Found on stones and plants in lakes and lake outflows.

Ithytrichia lamellaris

Larva up to 3 mm long and 1.1 mm across. Green with brown head and thorax. Head points forward. Rather delicate legs. Abdomen is compressed, swollen and fattest in the middle, with no gills. Lives in the open for the first four stages, but then spins a flat case with two light bands. It resembles a cucumber seed, up to 4 mm long and 1.5 mm across. The abdomen is twisted through 90°, and the case therefore lies flat on the surface. It feeds on diatoms; it is rare, but can be found among plants and stones in fast-flowing rivers.

Oxyethira sp.

Larva up to 3 mm long and 0.8 mm across. Green with brown head and thorax. Head points forward. Rather delicate legs. Abdomen is compressed, swollen and fattest in the middle, with no gills. Lives in the open for the first four stages, but then spins a bottle-shaped case, up to 4mm long and 1mm across. The pupal case is attached by spun thread to plants at all four corners. Common among plants and stones in ponds, lakes and slow-moving rivers.

Hydroptila sp.

Larva up to 3 mm. Green with brown head and thorax. Head points forward. Rather delicate legs. Abdomen is compressed, swollen and fattest in the middle, with no gills. Lives in the open for the first four stages, but then spins a bean- or mussel-shaped case of fine sand, up to 4 mm long. Common in lakes at depths of 1-2 metres.
One species, **H. sparsa**, may be seen scurrying over stones on the banks of slow-moving rivers.

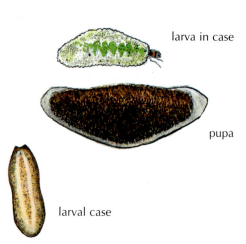

larva in case

pupa

larval case

Wormaldia occipitalis

Larva, up to 7 mm long and 1.5 mm across, has a long, slender head, pointing forwards. Yellow head and thorax. Whitish abdomen. Spins a bottle-like net up to 55 mm long and 7 mm across on the undersides of stones in springs with a strong current. The net filters out microorganisms from the water, and the larva sweeps them off with a flat labrum that unfolds and is edged with fine bristles. Occurs locally. This species is possibly a relict of warmer Atlantic climates.

larva x 5

Philopotamus montanus

Wingspan 18-21mm. Quite short antennae. Dark brown forewings with a characteristic pattern of golden spots and transverse bands. Flies May-July. Larva up to 22 mm long and 2.6 mm across. Shiny brown-yellow head and thorax with reddish spines. Abdomen is flattened and yellowish. Larva makes a net in fast-flowing springs, but is rare.

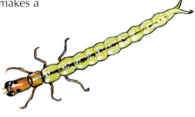

larva

Free-living caddis flies build a case in which to pupate. Case-bearers pupate in the larval case, while net-spinners pupate in a cocoon in their net.

Many caddis flies close their pupal cases at each end with a plate with tiny holes or a small crack in it to allow water to pass through. They are anchored to a solid object, often close to the water surface.

pupa

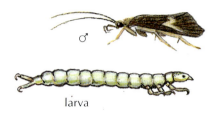

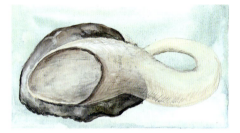

larva

net x 1/2

Neureclipsis bimaculata

Female wingspan is 18-21 mm; male 12-15 mm. Dark brown head and body with golden-grey hair. Forewings are grey with individual golden hairs and characteristic whitish-yellow marking. Hind wings are grey-black with dark veins. Flies May-September. Larva, up to 22 mm long and 2.5 mm across, has yellow head with small dark spots. Head flat and forward-pointing. Prothorax is yellow, with broad black back edge. Greenish abdomen with white lines along the sides. Terminal hooks are long and segmented. Spins a U-shaped tube. This is up to 15 cm long, and is found on plants and stones with its funnel-shaped opening facing the current. Larva feeds on plankton caught in the net. Usually found in moderately fast-flowing outflows from lakes.

Plectrocnemia conspersa

Larva up to 22 mm long and 3.5 mm across. Red-brown with dark forward-pointing head. Legs hairy; long, segmented terminal hooks. Spins a bag-shaped net rather like a spider's web between plants and stones. This is red-brown on the outside, shiny on the inside, and up to 10 mm long and 5 mm across. The larva is a predator, sitting in a thin tube leading from the back end of the net, and feeding on animals and other particles caught in the net. Uncommon, but found in springs and clean, cold streams, particularly in woods.

Polycentropus sp.

Larva up to 12 mm long and 2 mm across. Light brown, with forward-pointing head; powerful segmented terminal hooks with bristles. Spins a bag-shaped net like a swallows' nest. **P. flavomaculatus** is primarily found on stony lake shores, but also in slow- to moderately fast-moving rivers. **P. irroratus** is rare, but is usually found in moderately fast-flowing rivers.

Holocentropus dubius

Larva, up to 13 mm long and 2 mm across, has a yellowish head with a dark angular mark and small dark spots. Its legs have bristles, the abdomen has no gills, and the terminal hooks are long and segmented. Constructs a circular web with a long downward-pointing passage like an old-fashioned gramophone (His Master's Voice).

Cyrnus sp.

Larva, up to 15 mm long and 2 mm across, has a pale yellow forward-pointing head, and long, segmented anal claws. Spins a flat, funnel-shaped net on the undersides of leaves. Common in ponds, lakes and slow-moving water with abundant plant life. Several similar species.

Ecnomus tenellus

Larva, up to 8 mm long and 1.2 mm across, has yellow head with brown markings, pointing forward. All three thoracic segments and the back of the ninth abdominal segment have a hardened surface, and there are no gills on the abdomen. Bores through freshwater sponges. Rather local in Britain. Occurs locally in ponds and on muddy bottoms along lake-shores. Adult flies June-September.

x 6

Lype sp.

Larva up to 11 mm long, 1.5 mm across. Yellow head points forward and has a broad, dark, parallel-sided transverse band. Prothorax dark grey-brown with light spots. The rest of the body is pink, light brown underneath. Found in a curved gallery up to 75 mm long, scraped in submerged wood. The gallery is 5.5 mm wide at the front and 1.5 mm wide at the back. It is covered by a slime lid with small grains of sand clinging to it. Larva feeds on the wood. Common in streams and rivers, though easily overlooked. Larva moves fast, leaving the wood if it is picked up.

x 6

larva

Tinodes waeneri

Wingspan 12-18 mm. Head and thorax are dark brown, with golden hair. Powerful antennae are shorter than forewings. Forewings are light brown, very hairy at the edges, and often have a round, hairless spot. Hind wings are slender. Flies June-August.

Larva, up to 10 mm long and 1.2 mm across, has a yellowish or pale-green head, with brown markings. Prothorax has four large, pale-yellow spots. Terminal hooks have only one swollen segment. Spins a short tube covered in mud or fine sand, up to 60 mm long, on the upper sides of stones. Feeds on algae on the stones. Common on stones in lakes and slow-moving rivers.

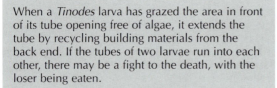

tube

larval head and prothorax x 15

When a *Tinodes* larva has grazed the area in front of its tube opening free of algae, it extends the tube by recycling building materials from the back end. If the tubes of two larvae run into each other, there may be a fight to the death, with the loser being eaten.

Tinodes pallidulus

Larva resembles *T. waeneri*, but is recognised by markings on the prothorax. Occurs locally on stones in streams and rivers. Very rare in Britain.

Phryganea bipunctata ♂

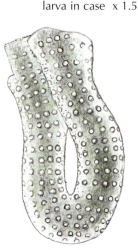

larva in case x 1.5

Phryganea **sp.**

Wingspan 39-60 mm. The largest caddis fly in the region. Female is larger than male. Forewings have large, grey, brown or dark-brown spots. Female's fore-wings also have a bold black band. Hind wings are grey or light brown. Flies June-August.

Larva, up to 40 mm long and 5 mm across, has a tilted head with dark markings. Abdomen is greenish with numerous long gills. Constructs a regular spiral case of equal-sized bits of wood or leaves. It is round in cross-section, and slightly narrower at the back end, up to 50 mm long and 9 mm across. A predator, crawling actively around plants; common in ponds, lakes and rivers.

The female *Phryganea* crawls down under water to lay eggs. The eggs are laid in a ring-shaped jelly mass on plant stems.

egg mass

All caddis flies have their mouth-parts and their legs free in the pupal stage. The middle pair of legs has swimming hairs. When the caddis fly is fully developed, it bites its way out of the pupal case, swims up to the surface, or over to plants or to the bank, crawls up onto dry land, and unfolds its wings.

Adult caddis flies may be seen in spring, summer or autumn, and some species even in winter. They normal-ly fly towards dusk, spending the day on vegetation near the water.
Caddis flies represent a very ancient order of insects. Wingprints have been found in rocks formed 200 million years ago.

♀

Trichostegia minor

Wingspan 26-30 mm. Grey head and prothorax, and large eyes. Forewings are broad and light grey, with broad black transverse bands and spots. Larva has a black, fork-shaped mark on its head, around a dark patch, and has no projection on the back of the first abdominal segment. Constructs a case of oblong plant fragments, occasionally forming a ring, up to 18 mm long and 2.5 mm across. It is a predator, occurring locally among plants in ponds.

larva in case

Hydropsyche pellucidula ♂

Hydropsyche pellucidula ♀

Hydropsyche angustipennis ♂

Hydropsyche angustipennis

Female wingspan is 21-27 mm; male is 18-21 mm. Black head and thorax with grey-yellow hair. Forewings are quite narrow, grey or dark grey, with golden-brown hair. Dark-grey hind wings. Flies May-September.
There are several, rather similar species, including **H. contubernalis.**

Hydropsyche contubernalis ♀

Larva up to 20 mm long and 2 mm across. Green or brown-grey, with brown forward-pointing head. All three thoracic segments have a brown surface, the second segment with distinct markings. Short, powerful legs; under the abdomen are two rows of shiny silver gill-tufts. Terminal hooks have a large, steeply-bowed claw and a tuft of black bristles. Larva spins a funnel-shaped tube of small stones, plant matter etc. with an opening at right angles to the direction of current and a back which shifts slightly with the current. The front end extends like a frame (approx. 10 mm in diameter) round a square-meshed net. Larva sits with abdomen in the tube and its hardened thorax facing the current, as it sweeps edible organic material from the net, from side to side. Common, often in large numbers, among stones in quite fast-flowing lake outflows.

'*Hydropsyche*' means the soul of the water.

larva with net

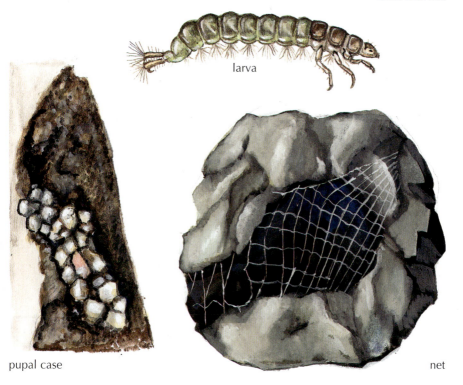

larva

pupal case

net

Molanna angustata

Female wingspan is 26-30 mm; male 19-26 mm. Black head. Red-brown thorax and abdomen. Forewings either transparent, with golden hair or dark grey to brown with distinct veins. Hind wings are greyish. Quite long legs. Male has long, hairy palps beneath its head. It rests slanting, with wings wrapped around itself, making it look like a withered blade of grass. Flies May-September.

Larva, up to 17 mm long and 2.7 mm across, has a black, fork-shaped mark on its head. Constructs a tube-shaped, slightly pointed case of sand, up to 26 mm long and 3 mm across, with a shield-shaped roof, which can be as much as 12 mm in diameter. The shape is possibly a protection against predators, and prevents the case sinking into the bottom or being overturned by waves or the current. Common on muddy sand bottoms in ponds and lakes, and slow-moving rivers, often at quite considerable depths. It can also be found in nutrient-poor lakes.

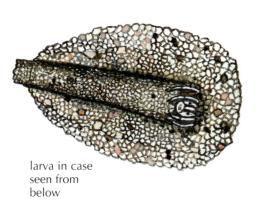

larva in case seen from below

Right: examples of caddis fly eggs. The eggs at the top, however, are of a mayfly, *Baetis* sp.

Athripsodes sp.

Wingspan 20-24 mm. Antennae have broad white rings on the inner half, and are more than double the length of the forewings, being longest in the male. Forewings are very long and narrow, with brown-grey or yellow hair and light spots. Hind wings are grey-black, more or less clear and iridescent. Flies June-September. Fast, zigzagging flight over water.

Larva, up to 11 mm long and 1.7 mm across, has a pale-yellow head, and its prothorax and mesothorax have small spots. Underside of head is black. Constructs a slightly curved and pointed case of black plant fragments mixed with sand, up to 19 mm long and 2.3 mm across. Feeds on algae and is common among plants in ponds and lakes. *A. cinereus* is found in moderately fast-flowing water and at lakeshores. *A. aterrimus* is common at the bottom of large rivers, in ponds and in deeper water in lakes.

larvae in cases

Ceraclea sp.

Wingspan 24-30 mm. Has very long, pale antennae and slender brown-grey wings. Larva up to 11 mm long and 2.2 mm across. Constructs a greenish or brownish case of silk, perhaps with individual plant fragments or grains of sand mixed in, up to 12 mm long and 2.5 mm across. Several almost identical species. Most gnaw winding tunnels in freshwater sponges, feeding on them, but causing them little damage. Found in lakes and moderately fast-flowing rivers. Non-British.

larva in case

♂

Mystacides longicornis

Wingspan 16-20 mm. Male's antennae twice as long as forewings; slightly shorter in female. Forewings are narrower than hind wings, golden yellow, and often have four dark transverse bands. Hind wings are grey-black. Head and thorax are shiny black. Male's palps are feathery and curved, and are held out to the side almost like a pair of legs. It is a good flier and is seen May-September.

Larva constructs a narrow, pointed, faintly curved case of sand, often with individual plant fragments and an outrigger, i.e. a small thin twig fastened on lengthwise. The case is up to 15 mm long and 2 mm across. Common among plants in ponds, lakes and slow-moving streams.

larva in case

Mystacides azurea ♂

larva in case

egg mass

Triaenodes bicolor

Female wingspan is 16-20 mm; male 13-15 mm. Antennae, with black rings, are more than twice the length of forewings. Often fly in large numbers, May-September.

Larva up to 13 mm long and 1.6 mm across. Constructs a straight, slender, pointed tube of oblong, equal-sized green plant fragments, put together in a spiral, up to 30 mm long and 2.5 mm across. Uses its long, bristle-covered back legs to jump forward through the water while remaining in its case. Common among plants in clumps of reeds in ponds and small lakes.

Eggs are laid in jelly-covered disc-shaped clumps on the underside of floating leaves.

Setodes sp.

Larva up to 8 mm long and 0.75 mm across. Constructs a long, narrow silken case, almost colourless or greenish, pointed and slightly curved. It swims among plants using its long, bristle-covered back legs and occurs locally in ponds, small lakes and very slow-moving water.

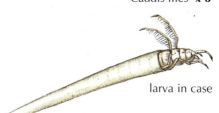

larva in case

Beraea sp.

Wingspan 10-12.5 mm. Head, thorax and abdomen black with brown-black hair. Wings are long-haired along the edges. Flies May-July.

Larva, up to 6 mm long and 1 mm across, has pink head and prothorax. Front edge of prothorax is brown. Curved and pointed case, up to 7 mm long and 1 mm across, is constructed of fine sand. Occurs locally, particularly in moss, on wet branches over water or among withered leaves along the banks of springs and woodland streams. Does not normally go into water.

larva in case

larva in case

Beraeodes minutus

Larva, up to 9 mm long and 1.2 mm across, has a pale-yellow head with a black forehead and a black band on each side. Prothorax is yellowish with small black spots. Case, up to 10 mm long and 1.5 mm across, is curved and pointed and constructed of fine sand. Occurs locally in small streams.

larva in case

Ernodes articularis

Larva up to 7 mm long, 1.1 mm across. Head is brown or red-brown, with yellow edges and spots. Constructs a curved case up to 10 mm long of fine sand. Found all year round, but particularly in spring, among moss in springs, small streams and marshes. Rare in Britain.

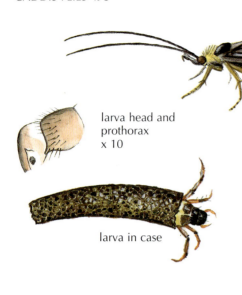

larva head and
prothorax
x 10

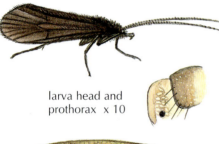

larva in case

Sericostoma personatum

Wingspan 24-32 mm. Forewings are
grey-black with yellow-brown hair.
Hind wings are almost black with
black veins. Head and prothorax are
golden brown or orange. Flies June-
September.
Larva, up to 12 mm long and 2.5 mm
across, has prothorax with pointed
front corners. Builds a smooth and
somewhat curved case of fine sand, 15
mm long and 3 mm across. Common
in springs and streams, and more rarely
in lakes.

Notidobia ciliaris

Wingspan 20-24 mm. Black wings;
head and prothorax have black hair.
Flies May-June.
Larva up to 17 mm long and 3 mm
across, has brown head; its prothorax
has yellowish spots and rounded front
corners. Constructs a gently curved
case of sand, up to 18 mm long and
3.5 mm across. Found mainly in rivers
and on the shores of large lakes.

larva head and
prothorax x 10

larva in case

Lepidostoma hirtum

Larva up to 11 mm long and 2 mm
across. When young, it constructs a
smooth, straight and pointed tube of
sand. When older it constructs a
straight, pointed case of plant fragments, square in cross-section, especially towards the front. Occurs mainly
in streams and rivers with abundant
plant life; also in the splash zone of
large lakes.

larva in case

Brachycentrus subnubilus

Wingspan 11-16 mm. Black body. Head and prothorax have grey-yellow hair. Forewings are grey with numerous pale-yellow spots more or less joined together. Male is more boldly spotted than female. Hind wings are grey-brown with dark-brown veins. Larva, up to 12 mm long and 2.5 mm across, has yellow-brown head; prothorax has dark bands and spots. When young it constructs a square case of plant fragments, positioned across rather than along the case. Older larvae have cases made only of silk, with rounded edges at the front. Case is up to 12 mm long and 3 mm across. Feeds on small particles filtered from the water with bristles on the inner edges of its middle and hind legs. Common in clean, running water.

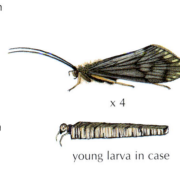

x 4

young larva in case

Brachycentrus maculatus

Larva, up to 11 mm long and 1.7 mm across, has yellow-brown head; prothorax has darker sections. Abdomen is green. Constructs a straight, conical case of fine sand, up to 20 mm long and 1.8 mm across. It rests with its middle and back legs outspread facing the current, and catches small particles in the bristly edges of its tibiae. Occurs locally on the continent, occasionally in large numbers, in streams and rivers with a strong current and clean water. Non-British.

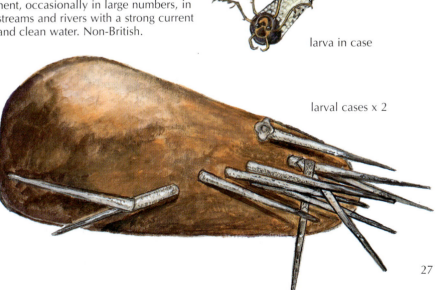

larva in case

larval cases x 2

27

CADDIS FLIES x 3

Crunoecia irrorata

Wingspan 11-14 mm. Light- or dark-brown body with golden-brown hair. Forewings have golden-brown hair, sprinkled with black. Hind wings are greyish and iridescent. Flies July-September.

Larva up to 7 mm long and 1.6 mm across. Constructs first a straight, pointed case of fine sand; later it makes a square, pointed case of plant fragments, which are gnawed so they fit together. Inside the case is round, up to 9 mm long and 2 mm across. Found locally, well camouflaged among leaves near fast-flowing springs in woodland. Larva does not normally go under water.

older larva in case

Lasiocephala basalis

Larva, up to 11 mm long and 2 mm across, has thick forelegs, with middle and hind legs being twice as long and thin. Constructs a curved, pointed and rather rough case out of sand, up to 25 mm long and 2 mm across. Rare, found in rivers and streams.

larva in case

Silo pallipes, pairing

larva in case

Occasionally one comes across caddis fly cases of the genera *Silo* or *Goera*, with a long, twisted band coming from them. This is part of a parasitic wasp larva, **Agriotypus armatus,** which consumes the caddis and then pupates in its case. See page 65.

parasitic wasp in larval case

Silo pallipes

Wingspan 14-18 mm. Male has black body; female's is lighter and brownish. Male's forewings are dark brown to black; female's are light brown with a golden sheen. Hind wings of male are brown-black with black veins and coarse black hair along a fold. Female's are lighter and have no fold. Flies June-August.

Larva up to 10 mm long and 2 mm across. Constructs a case of sand with small stones along the sides for ballast. The stones are the same size or smaller than the tube's inner diameter. The case is up to 12 mm long and 9 mm across. Feeds on algae scraped off stones.

Common on stony bottoms of fast-flowing streams and rivers.

A similar species, **S. nigricornis**, which lives in springs, has a red head and builds slightly larger cases.

Goera pilosa

Larva, up to 14 mm long and 3 mm across, has a vertically-positioned head that can be pulled into the prothorax. Case is constructed of sand with large stones along the sides for ballast. Some of the stones are wider than the inner diameter of the tube, which is up to 16 mm long and 20 mm across. Feeds on algae scraped off stones. This genus is common on stony lakeshores and on stones in moderately fast-flowing streams.

larva in case

Apatania muliebris

Larva up to 7 mm long. Constructs a slightly curved and pointed case, with fine sand on the top and bottom, and coarse sand at the sides. Larva grows throughout the summer, seals its case to make it a pupal case in September, but does not pupate until spring.

larva in case x 6

This species is a late glacial cold relict that cannot tolerate a water temperature above 10° for lengthy periods. Rare.

Ironoquia dubia

Larva, up to 18 mm long, has gill tufts with 10 or more gills in each one. Constructs a curved and almost cylindrical case of irregularly-shaped leaf fragments, up to 23 mm long. Occurs locally in slow-moving streams with abundant plant life. Very rare in Britain.

gill tufts of larva x 6

larval case

Ecclisopteryx dalecarlica

Larva, up to 8 mm long, has black eyes on a dark, hairy head, which looks a bit like the head of a miniature mouse. Constructs a gently curved case up to 10 mm long of fine sand. Non-British.

larva in case x 6

29

Three examples of larval cases of the genus *Limnephilus*, made of a variety of plant matter. There are many species of *Limnephilus*, and it is very difficult to tell the larvae apart.

x 2

larva in case

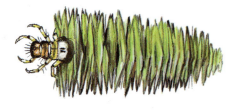

Limnephilus stigma

Larva builds a case of green leaf fragments of uneven size, across the longitudinal axis, 20-25 mm long and 8-20 mm across. Common among plants in bogs, ponds, lakes and slow-moving water with a certain amount of leaf matter on the bottom.

larva in case

Limnephilus sparsus

Larva up to 17 mm long and 4 mm across. Constructs a pointed case of fine plant fragments placed across the longitudinal axis, up to 16 mm long and 4 mm across. Common in ponds and lakes with abundant plant life.

Limnephilus binotatus

Larva up to 20 mm long and 4 mm across. Constructs an even, smooth and pointed case of small plant fragments, up to 20 mm long and 4 mm across. Common in ponds and lakes with abundant plant life.

larva in case

Limnephilus rhombicus

Wingspan 28-35 mm. Fairly small, parchment-like forewings, with little hair. They have dark patches, and a glassy rhomboid spot in the middle of the wings. Hind wings are broader. Larva, up to 25 mm long and 4.5 mm across, has a black, vase-shaped patch on the forehead. Constructs a clumsy case of small stones, twigs, pieces of reeds, and snail shells and shell fragments, up to 27 mm long and 6.5 mm across. The snails are often alive but unable to escape. Very common in ponds, lakes and ditches with abundant plant life.

In a similar species, **L. flavicornis**, the patch on the forehead looks like a stemmed bowl. Builds a similar case, but the narrower rear end is constructed of finer fragments.

larval head markings x 6
larva in case
larval case of *L. flavicornis*

Limnephilus extricatus

Larva, up to 14 mm long and 2 mm across, has yellow-brown head, prothorax and mesothorax. Constructs a bowed, almost cylindrical case, with a rounded rear end, out of fine sand, up to 16 mm long and 3.7 mm across. Common in slow-moving, clean water.

A similar species, **L. bipunctatus**, builds a similar but slightly larger case of coarser sand. It lives in ponds, lakes and slow-moving water.

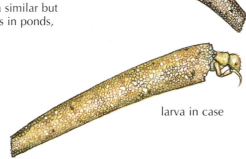

larva in case

Limnephilus vittatus

Larva up to 12 mm long and 2 mm across. Constructs a slightly curved, pointed case of fine sand mixed with small plant fragments, with an oblique, arched indentation on the underside, up to 22 mm long and 2.2 mm across. Common in ponds and lakes.

larva in case

larval case x 2

Glyphotaelius pellucidus

Eggs are laid on leaves above the water, surrounded by jelly, which swells up. In rainy weather, or after the evening dew has fallen, the larvae drop into the water. Larva is up to 23 mm long and 4 mm across. Constructs a large, flat case of broad leaf fragments, up to 60 mm long and 30 mm across. Common in ponds, small lakes and ditches with withered leaves. A similar (non-British) species, **G. punctatolineatus**, constructs the same kind of case, but camouflages it in winter with long leaves along the length of the case.

young and older larva in case

larval head marking x 6

Anabolia sp.

Larva has a toadstool-like mark on its head between two large wavy lines. Constructs a case of coarse sand with several small twigs as outriggers, which can be over twice as long as the case itself. These extend it, protecting the larva from small fish. The case itself is up to 25 mm long and 4 mm across. Common in streams, lakes and rivers.

pupal case x 1

Stenophylax sp.

Larva constructs a case of rotting pieces of wood or bark, often with a single twig as outrigger.
Pupal cases are made of small stones, and attached to stones. Fairly common in streams.

above: examples of egg masses of the family *Limnephilidae*, the caddis flies on these and the preceding pages

Parachiona picicornis

Larva constructs a pointed and bowed case of sand, up to 12 mm long and 3.5 mm across. Rare, found in springs with sandy, gravelly bottoms. Non-British.

larva in case

Grammotaulius nigropunctata

Larva, up to 28 mm long and 5 mm across, has yellowish head and prothorax and yellow legs. Constructs a straight, pointed case of long stems and blades of grass, up to 50 mm long and 6 mm across. Common among grasses in puddles, small ponds and ditches.

larva in case x 1.5

Phacopteryx brevipennis

Larva up to 12 mm long and 2 mm across. Constructs a triangular case of pieces of bark or of flat, round leaf fragments, especially beech leaves, up to 20 mm long and 6 mm across. Found in ponds with withered leaves in woods. Rare in Britain.

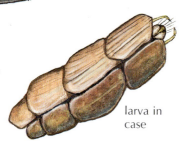

larva in case

ALDER FLIES

Alder flies have two pairs of large, almost identical wings with a pronounced network of black veins, held roofwise over the body at rest. They are rather poor fliers. They have large eyes, and long, thin antennae. The adults eat small amounts of pollen from flowers, while the larvae are predators. There are three European species, but only two species occur in Britain.

Alder Fly *Sialis lutaria*

Body approx. 20 mm, wingspan 22-34 mm. Body short and powerful, dark brown or black. Brownish or greyish wings. Female lays up to 2,000 eggs in dense masses on branches and leaves close over water. Very common near streams, large ponds and lakes in early summer, when it moves or flies sluggishly and rather cautiously around the vegetation. It lives only a short time, eating only a little pollen if anything.

adult with egg mass

larva

Larva, up to 25 mm, has a large head with powerful, curved mandibles. Its head and thorax are hard, with dark and light markings; its abdomen is soft and somewhat lighter in colour. It has three pairs of bristly legs and one pair of feathery tracheal gills on each abdominal segment except the last, which has only one long feathery thread. It is an efficient predator, living primarily on the larvae of non-biting midges, worms and other small animals. It can swim but does so only rarely, normally living buried in silt. Common; can be found both shallow and deep water in lakes. Development takes 1-2 years. The grown larva digs itself about 7 cm down into the soil on land in order to pupate. After 2-3 weeks the pupa crawls up and transforms itself into the adult insect.

The larvae of two similar species are found sheltered from the current behind stones in streams and rivers: **S. nigripes** and **S. fuliginosa.**

LACEWINGS

Lacewings have two pairs of large, broad, often powerful wings, held steeply roofwise over the abdomen at rest. Most fly rather poorly. They have a long, soft body, large eyes and long, thin antennae. Most are predators, feeding primarily on aphids and other small insects, while others feed on honeydew, pollen etc. The larvae are predators.

right: *Osmylus fulvicephalus*
below: Spongefly

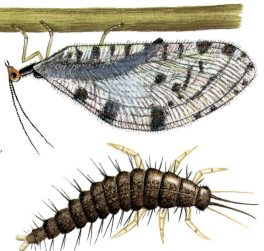

Spongefly
Sisyra fuscata

Wingspan 12-14 mm, brown or pitch black, front part of body shiny. Antennae are black, long and thin like a string of beads. Wings are large, broad, shiny and brownish. Common among plants by lakes and rivers, where it catches small insects, May-August. Often seen in small swarms. Flight is slow; it plays dead if caught.
Larva, up to 5 mm, is yellow-green with two long, stiff antennae, with which it moves itself along in small jumps. Two rows segmented tracheal gills beneath the abdomen. The mouthparts have evolved as sucking tubes. Feeds by sucking the soft parts of freshwater sponges and moss animals. Pupation takes place in a small, yellow-brown cocoon on rushes and other aquatic plants, bridge piers, tree trunks etc. Overwinters as pupa. There are three British species.

Osmylus fulvicephalus larva

Largest lacewing in Britain, with a wingspan of 42-48 mm. Head is red-brown to dark brown. Long, thin antennae. Black body. Forewings have brown-black patches along the edge and are brightly iridescent. Occurs locally near springs, streams and rivers, particularly in shady woods, under bridges etc, June-July.
Larva, up to 20 mm, is dark brown, flat and elongated, with strong bristles. Mandibles are in the form of sucking tubes. Primarily found in damp moss, where it hunts larvae of flies and mosquitoes. Overwinters as larva.

larva

DRAGONFLIES

Dragonflies are large insects with a mobile head and large eyes. The thorax is short and broad, with three pairs of long, hairy legs with powerful claws. They have two pairs of large, often clear wings with a distinct vein network, and a long, segmented abdomen. They are predators. Dragonflies undergo partial metamorphosis. The eggs develop into nymphs, generally called larvae. These catch their prey with their labium, 'the mask', shaped like segmented forceps, which shoot forward in front of the head. The metamorphosis to adult takes place over water, often on plants, by night or early in the morning.

Dragonflies are divided into two groups: *true dragonflies* and *damselflies.* Approx. 40 species in Britain.

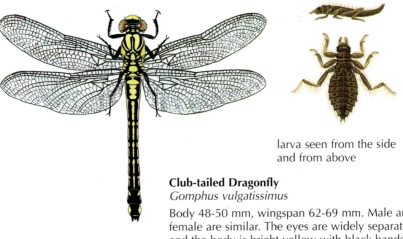

larva seen from the side and from above

Club-tailed Dragonfly
Gomphus vulgatissimus

Body 48-50 mm, wingspan 62-69 mm. Male and female are similar. The eyes are widely separated, and the body is bright yellow with black bands and spots. Occurs locally in Britain, notably on mature rivers in the west and south, May-July.

Larva, up to 30 mm, is broad, flat and yellow-grey. It is very hairy and has powerful digging legs, particularly the two front pairs. The hind legs are shorter than the abdomen, and the wing sheaths lie parallel over the back. Short antennae. Lives buried in the splash zone of large lakes or in river bottoms.

Golden-ringed Dragonfly
Cordulegaster boltoni
Body 75-83 mm. Wingspan 88-104
mm. One of the largest dragonflies in
Britain. Male and female are very
similar. Prothorax is black with yellow
stripes, the thorax has yellow spots and
the abdomen has narrow yellow rings.
Common in heaths and moors of the
south and west of Britain, June-July.
Larva, up to 50 mm, is hairy, flat and
elongated. Abdomen is spindle-shaped
and mottled. The mask is bowl-shaped,
and the antennae are short. Lives
buried at the bottom of the water.
Development takes 4-5 years.
Another large dragonfly is the **Emperor
Dragonfly**, *Anax imperator*. Its body is
up to 82 mm long, and its wingspan is
approx. 110 mm. Common in parts of
southern Britain, and south from
southern Scandinavia.

larva

True dragonflies catch their prey on
the wing. They are among the best
and fastest flying insects, and can fly
at 35-40 km per hour. They can fly
vertically and backwards, and can
throw themselves to the side. Dragonflies often fly long distances, and
some species undertake migrations.

True dragonflies feed on other insects, particularly flies, wasps, mayflies, butterflies and occasionally
other dragonflies. The abdomen is
rather fat, occasionally broad and
flat. The fore- and hind wings differ
markedly, and are held flat and at
right angles to the body at rest. The
larvae are large and broad. They
have no gill lamellae, breathing
through the skin and by means of
gills in the rectum.

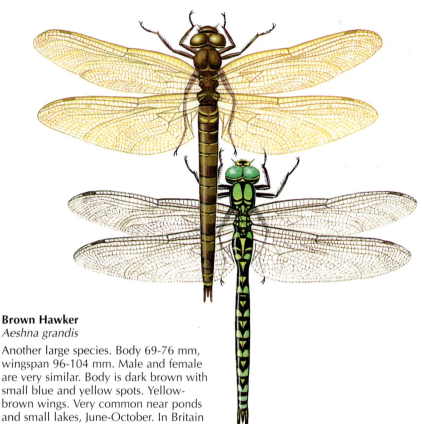

Brown Hawker
Aeshna grandis

Another large species. Body 69-76 mm,
wingspan 96-104 mm. Male and female
are very similar. Body is dark brown with
small blue and yellow spots. Yellow-
brown wings. Very common near ponds
and small lakes, June-October. In Britain
mainly lowland England and Ireland.
Larva, up to 47 mm, is long and slender,
with a flat mask and large eyes. Can
catch large insects in the water.

Southern Hawker
Aeshna cyanea

Body 71-74 mm, wingspan 97-110
mm. Male has blue eyes and yellow-
green and blue spots, particularly on
the abdominal tip. Female has yellow-
brown eyes and yellow and green
spots on its body. Common near small
lakes and ponds, June-October. In
Britain very common in lowland England and Wales.
Larva up to 45 mm.

Aeshna sp. larvae

True dragonfly males maintain territories near water. Strange males are chased away, often in fierce battles.

Although dragonflies are very large, they weigh very little, their bodies containing many air spaces. The largest weighs less than one gram.

Aeshna sp. larva

Common Hawker
Aeshna juncea

Body 74-76 mm, wingspan 88-96 mm. Rear of head is black with a small yellow spot behind each eye. Abdomen of male is black with large blue and smaller yellow spots. Large abdominal spots are more yellowish in the female. Fairly common near ponds and lakes from June to October and usually spotted near nutrient-poor lakes, often in large numbers. Common in central and northern Europe; in Britain and Ireland mainly in the west and north.

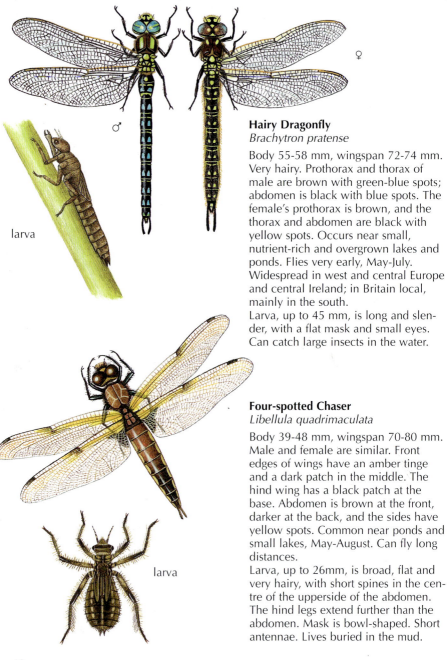

♀

♂

larva

Hairy Dragonfly
Brachytron pratense

Body 55-58 mm, wingspan 72-74 mm.
Very hairy. Prothorax and thorax of
male are brown with green-blue spots;
abdomen is black with blue spots. The
female's prothorax is brown, and the
thorax and abdomen are black with
yellow spots. Occurs near small,
nutrient-rich and overgrown lakes and
ponds. Flies very early, May-July.
Widespread in west and central Europe
and central Ireland; in Britain local,
mainly in the south.
Larva, up to 45 mm, is long and slender, with a flat mask and small eyes.
Can catch large insects in the water.

Four-spotted Chaser
Libellula quadrimaculata

Body 39-48 mm, wingspan 70-80 mm.
Male and female are similar. Front
edges of wings have an amber tinge
and a dark patch in the middle. The
hind wing has a black patch at the
base. Abdomen is brown at the front,
darker at the back, and the sides have
yellow spots. Common near ponds and
small lakes, May-August. Can fly long
distances.
Larva, up to 26mm, is broad, flat and
very hairy, with short spines in the centre of the upperside of the abdomen.
The hind legs extend further than the
abdomen. Mask is bowl-shaped. Short
antennae. Lives buried in the mud.

larva

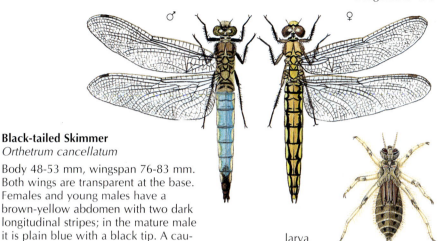

Black-tailed Skimmer
Orthetrum cancellatum

Body 48-53 mm, wingspan 76-83 mm.
Both wings are transparent at the base.
Females and young males have a
brown-yellow abdomen with two dark
longitudinal stripes; in the mature male
it is plain blue with a black tip. A cau-
tious and fast-flying dragonfly, often
seen far from water, which frequently
rests on stones or bare earth. Occurs
locally near lakes, large ponds and
gravel pits, June-August. In Britain,
mainly in southern England.
Larva, up to 26 mm, is fairly broad and
very hairy, but has no spines on the
rear segments.

larva

Broad-bodied Chaser *Libellula depressa*

Body 40-47 mm, wingspan 74-78 mm.
Abdomen is very broad, brown with yellow side-spots in the female and young
males, blue with yellow side-spots in the
mature male. Both wings have brown
patches at the base. Fairly common, particularly in southern England and Wales.
Prefers shallow, sunny ponds, May-July.
Larva, up to 25 mm, resembles larva of
Four-spotted Chaser (see p. 40).

empty larval skin

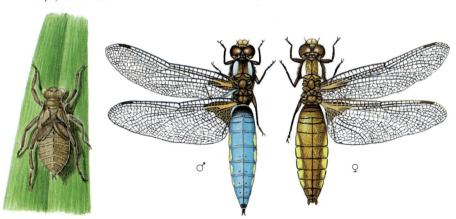

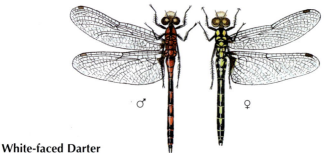

White-faced Darter
Leucorrhinia dubia

Body 34-39 mm, wingspan 52-58 mm. A small and delicate dragonfly with a white face. Hind wing has a brown-black patch at the base. Female has a black body with yellow spots. Body of male has red spots. Locally common in northern Europe, near nutrient-poor, acidic ponds and lakes, May-July. In Britain it is rare, only known from a few sites, with a stronghold in the Scottish highlands.

Larva, up to 22 mm, is broad with a yellow mid-line and yellow spots on the upperside of abdomen. Underside has broad, dark bands.

It is thought that dragonflies use their short antennae as a kind of speedometer. When wind resistance pushes them back, the dragonfly can tell how fast it is flying.

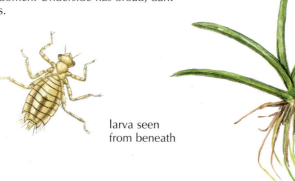

larva seen
from beneath

shoreweed

The development from egg to adult dragonfly takes a long time – up to five years. The larvae slowly change shape with each moult, and it is only in the last stage just before metamorphosis that they can be identified with any certainty.

Dragonflies' eyes are composed of around 30,000 simple units (ommatidia). A dragonfly can see in front, behind, up and down at the same time, so it is almost impossible to surprise one.

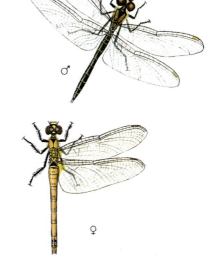

Black Darter
Sympetrum danae

A small dragonfly – body 28-34 mm, wingspan 43-52 mm. The mature male is plain black above. The female is orange-brown with black spots and stripes, and wings with a small yellow patch at the base. Fairly common, especially in the north and west of Britain and Ireland, near nutrient-poor ponds, lakes and bogs; occasionally found in very large numbers, July-October.

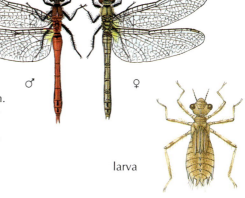

Ruddy Darter
Sympetrum sanguineum

Body 33-36 mm, wingspan 50-59 mm. A small dragonfly, with wings that are yellow at the base. Abdomen of male is blood red. That of female is brown-yellow, with thin black longitudinal stripes. Catches small insects only. Common near ponds and lakes, June-October. Several similar species. Larva, up to 17 mm, is broad with strong spines on the upperside of the abdomen and long spines on the sides of the rearmost abdominal segment. However these are not apparent to the naked eye. Hind legs are longer than abdomen.

larva

The larvae of true dragonflies can thrust water out of their rectums with such force that they rocket forward through the water.

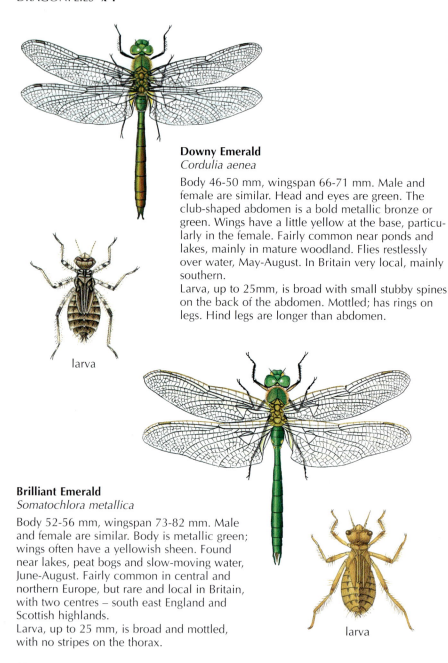

Downy Emerald
Cordulia aenea

Body 46-50 mm, wingspan 66-71 mm. Male and female are similar. Head and eyes are green. The club-shaped abdomen is a bold metallic bronze or green. Wings have a little yellow at the base, particularly in the female. Fairly common near ponds and lakes, mainly in mature woodland. Flies restlessly over water, May-August. In Britain very local, mainly southern.

Larva, up to 25mm, is broad with small stubby spines on the back of the abdomen. Mottled; has rings on legs. Hind legs are longer than abdomen.

larva

Brilliant Emerald
Somatochlora metallica

Body 52-56 mm, wingspan 73-82 mm. Male and female are similar. Body is metallic green; wings often have a yellowish sheen. Found near lakes, peat bogs and slow-moving water, June-August. Fairly common in central and northern Europe, but rare and local in Britain, with two centres – south east England and Scottish highlands.

Larva, up to 25 mm, is broad and mottled, with no stripes on the thorax.

larva

Damselflies

Damselflies fly rather slowly. They feed primarily on aphids, mosquitoes, mayflies, caddis flies and occasionally other damselflies, mostly catching prey that they find in vegetation. Their eyes are almost spherical, and they have a long, thin abdomen and identical fore- and hind wings, which are generally held upright together over the back at rest.
The larvae are long and slender, with three 'gill lamellae' on the abdominal tip. They swim by slow, swaying movements.

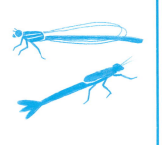

Emerald Damselfly
Lestes sponsa

Body 35-38 mm, wingspan 42-46 mm. Male's body is shiny green, blue or green-black. The two front and two back abdominal segments are light blue. Female's body is green, but can have a coppery tinge. Wings are often held out obliquely to the side at rest. Common near ponds, lakes and ditches with stagnant water and abundant plant growth, June-September. Larva, up to 27 mm, has rather slender gill lamellae; often has dark transverse bands.

larva

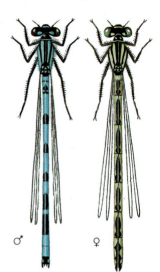

Common Blue Damselfly *Enallagma cyathigerum*

Body 30-33 mm, wingspan 36-40 mm. Male is blue with black markings and has a black 'ace of spades' mark at the front of the abdomen. Female is generally grey-green and black and has a strong barb under the penultimate abdominal segment. Common near ponds and lakes, May-September. Can occasionally occur in very large numbers near nutrient-poor and slightly acidic lakes.
Larva, up to 20 mm, has relatively short gill lamellae with 1-3 narrow transverse bands.

larva

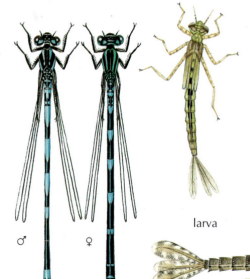

Variable Damselfly
Coenagrion pulchellum

Body 32-36 mm, wingspan 38-50 mm. Black prothorax, with blue stripes in the male and more greenish stripes in the female. Abdomen has black and blue transverse stripes. Male has a Y-shaped mark on the upperside of the second abdominal segment. Common near ponds, lakes and rivers with abundant plant life, May-August. Several similar species. Common in Ireland; in Britain scattered, mainly in southern England and Wales.
Larva, up to 19 mm, has sharply divided and blunt-ended gill lamellae. Femur have distinct rings.

larva

When pairing, the male perches on the female's thorax, arches his abdomen and grasps the female behind her head using his abdominal claspers. Then he straightens his abdomen, and the two fly in tandem until they are both ready to mate. During the actual copulation, the female bends her abdomen up to the male's second or third abdominal segment, from where the sperm is collected. This is called a copulation wheel. Damselflies mate on plants, while true dragonflies usually mate in the air. The eggs are laid in water or inserted into plant stems. Some dragonflies lay their eggs on the bank, where they hatch the following spring when the bank floods.

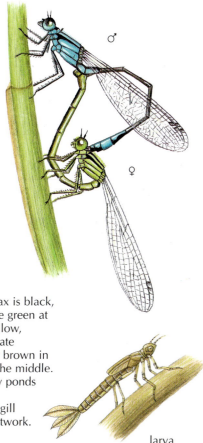

Blue-tailed Damselfly *Ischnura elegans*

Body 30-33 mm, wingspan 33-37 mm. Prothorax is black, with two longitudinal bands that in the male are green at first and later blue, and in the female, green-yellow, orange or violet. Black abdomen. The penultimate abdominal segment is blue in the male, blue or brown in the female. Male's abdomen is very slender in the middle. Very common near all kinds of water, even new ponds and brackish pools, May-September.
Larva, up to 20 mm, has long, slender, pointed gill lamellae, and a very fine and dense tracheal network.

larva

The three gill lamellae under the abdomen of damselflies function both as breathing organs and in swimming, though the animals can usually survive without them provided plenty of oxygen is available.

traces of damselfly egg-laying on a water-lily leaf

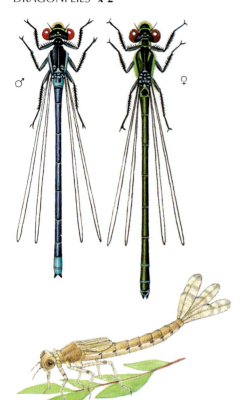

Red-eyed Damselfly
Erythromma najas

Body 35-38 mm, wingspan 45-52 mm. Eyes of male are normally red; abdomen is metallic dark blue, with the first and two last segments light blue. Abdomen of female is metallic bronze green on the upperside and yellow on the underside. The best fliers among damselflies. Spotted locally flying low over large ponds, lakes and rivers with floating leaves, May-August, where the male often maintains territory.

Larva, up to 29 mm, has a spiny point in the rear corners of each abdominal segment. Gill lamellae are clearly divided into two, and the outermost section has three dark transverse bands.

larva

bog arum
with empty
larval skin of
damselfly

Damselfly larvae can swim through water in a wriggling movement by clamping their legs close to their body and moving their gill lamellae from side to side.

Large Red Damselfly
Pyrrhosoma nymphula

Body 34-37 mm, wingspan 45-50 mm.
Distinctive red and black pattern on
abdomen. Male has narrow black rings
on the abdominal segments. In the
female these rings are broader, and the
rear third of the abdomen is almost
completely black. Thorax is black with
red stripes. Common near ponds, clean
lakes and quiet streams, May-August.
Larva, up to 19 mm, has short pointed
gill lamellae with a distinctive X-
shaped mark.

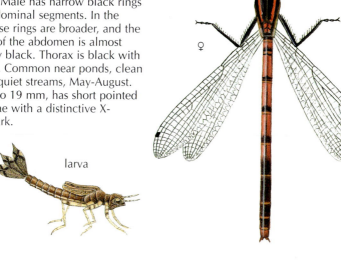

♀

larva

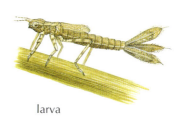

♂

White-legged Damselfly
Platycnemis pennipes

Body 36-38 mm, wingspan 43-48 mm. The middle
and hind pairs of legs are white and very broad. Prothorax is yellowish with black stripes. Male is often
light blue with dark abdominal tip. Female is light
green-yellow, often with thin black longitudinal
stripes in pairs on the abdomen. Rather local, found
near lakes and slow-moving rivers with abundant
plant growth, June-August. In Britain, found only in
southern England and Wales.
Larva, up to 19 mm, has gill lamellae ending in a
long point and covered with long thin bristles.

larva

49

Demoiselles

Demoiselles are large damselflies with metallic bodies and (in the males) coloured wing patches. The female has a small clear patch at the front edge of the wings, a pseudo-wing-mark. They have long legs, with the hind legs longer than the forelegs. They lay eggs in plants in oxygen-rich running water. The larvae have stiff, triangular gill lamellae. Other damselflies have clear wings with a wing-mark, and a dark patch by the front edge of both wings, but their legs are not as long as those of demoiselles, and their hind legs are not longer than the forelegs.

♂

empty larval skin on reed

Beautiful Demoiselle *Calopteryx virgo*

Body 45-48 mm, wingspan 65-72 mm. Large damselfly. Male is shiny green or blue, with blue wings. Female is bronze-coloured, the abdominal tip is brownish or reddish, and the wings are browner than those of the Banded Demoiselle. Lays eggs in plants in quite fast-flowing water with a gravelly, sandy bottom. Locally common, mainly in south and south-west Britain and Ireland, June-August.
Larva, up to 32mm, resembles larva of Banded Demoiselle (see p. 51). Moves around in vegetation very stiffly, rather like a praying mantis.

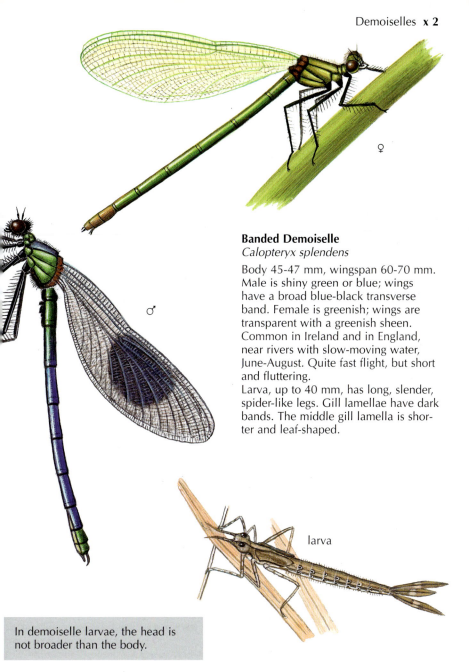

Banded Demoiselle
Calopteryx splendens
Body 45-47 mm, wingspan 60-70 mm.
Male is shiny green or blue; wings
have a broad blue-black transverse
band. Female is greenish; wings are
transparent with a greenish sheen.
Common in Ireland and in England,
near rivers with slow-moving water,
June-August. Quite fast flight, but short
and fluttering.
Larva, up to 40 mm, has long, slender,
spider-like legs. Gill lamellae have dark
bands. The middle gill lamella is shorter and leaf-shaped.

larva

In demoiselle larvae, the head is
not broader than the body.

MAYFLIES

The adult lives of mayflies last from just a few hours to a couple of weeks, and they do not feed. They have long tail filaments and two pairs of clear wings, held vertically or partially unfolded at rest. The front wings are large and tri-angular. The hind wings are considerably smaller, and are completely absent in some species. They fly reasonably confidently but cannot cope with winds. The adults are usually spotted at dusk, the males on their mating flights, or females flying upstream to lay their eggs. Mayflies have two or three thin tail filaments at their rear end, and very long forelegs, used for grasping the female during mating. Mayflies undergo partial metamorphosis. The nymphs have three tail filaments, short antennae and gills on the abdomen. They usually feed on algae and detritus. The nymph develops into a sub-imago, which resembles the adult mayfly, but is duller (see p. 55). There are about 200 species in Europe, some 50 or so in Britain.

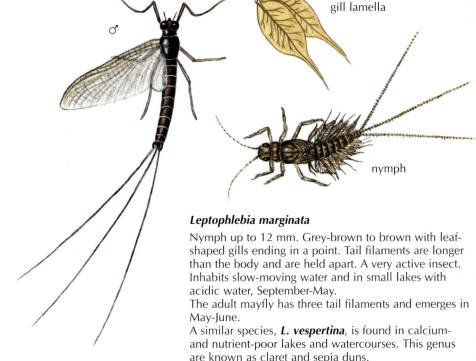

gill lamella

nymph

Leptophlebia marginata

Nymph up to 12 mm. Grey-brown to brown with leaf-shaped gills ending in a point. Tail filaments are longer than the body and are held apart. A very active insect. Inhabits slow-moving water and in small lakes with acidic water, September-May.

The adult mayfly has three tail filaments and emerges in May-June.

A similar species, **L. vespertina**, is found in calcium- and nutrient-poor lakes and watercourses. This genus are known as claret and sepia duns.

Turkey Brown
Paraleptophlebia sp.

Nymph up to 12 mm. Grey-brown with slender gill lamellae, ending in a point. Occurs locally in streams and rivers, September-June.
The adult mayfly has three tail filaments. Male's abdomen is whitish and almost transparent at the front. Flies May-June.

nymph

♀

gill lamella

Blue-winged Olive Mayfly *Ephemerella ignita*

Nymph up to 10 mm. Light sand-coloured to dark brown, and fairly mottled. Legs and tail filaments have dark bands and stiff bristles. On the upperside of the abdomen are five pairs of stiff gill lamellae, which overlap but do not protrude at the sides. The fifth pair of gills is covered by the fourth. May occur in very large numbers among plants in fast-flowing rivers, May-October.
The adult mayfly has three tail filaments. The male has eyes divided in two, of which the upper part is large and spherical. Flies June-October.

nymph

♂

53

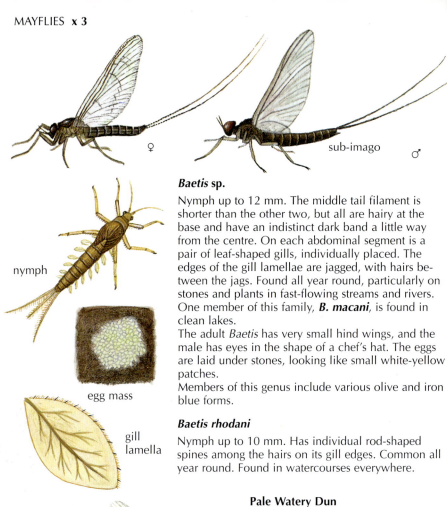

♀

sub-imago ♂

nymph

egg mass

gill
lamella

Baetis sp.

Nymph up to 12 mm. The middle tail filament is
shorter than the other two, but all are hairy at the
base and have an indistinct dark band a little way
from the centre. On each abdominal segment is a
pair of leaf-shaped gills, individually placed. The
edges of the gill lamellae are jagged, with hairs between the jags. Found all year round, particularly on
stones and plants in fast-flowing streams and rivers.
One member of this family, **B. macani**, is found in
clean lakes.

The adult *Baetis* has very small hind wings, and the
male has eyes in the shape of a chef's hat. The eggs
are laid under stones, looking like small white-yellow
patches.

Members of this genus include various olive and iron
blue forms.

Baetis rhodani

Nymph up to 10 mm. Has individual rod-shaped
spines among the hairs on its gill edges. Common all
year round. Found in watercourses everywhere.

Pale Watery Dun
Centroptilum luteolum

Nymph up to 8 mm. Sand-coloured,
with a dark pattern on the abdomen.
Pointed gill lamellae. Tail filaments are
hairy from the middle onwards, with
thin, dark rings up to the middle. Common all year round, but especially in
summer among plants in sandy-
bottomed lakes and rivers.

The adult mayfly has two tail filaments
and small, ribbon-shaped hind wings.
Male has eyes divided in two. Seen
May-October.

nymph

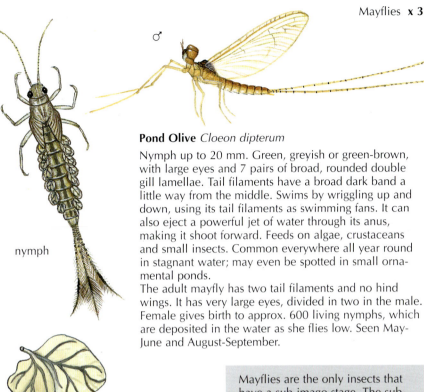

nymph

Pond Olive *Cloeon dipterum*

Nymph up to 20 mm. Green, greyish or green-brown, with large eyes and 7 pairs of broad, rounded double gill lamellae. Tail filaments have a broad dark band a little way from the middle. Swims by wriggling up and down, using its tail filaments as swimming fans. It can also eject a powerful jet of water through its anus, making it shoot forward. Feeds on algae, crustaceans and small insects. Common everywhere all year round in stagnant water; may even be spotted in small ornamental ponds.

The adult mayfly has two tail filaments and no hind wings. It has very large eyes, divided in two in the male. Female gives birth to approx. 600 living nymphs, which are deposited in the water as she flies low. Seen May-June and August-September.

gill lamella

Mayflies go through more moults in the nymphal stage than most other insects. *Cloeon dipterum*, for example, develops over two years and moults 24 times before reaching adulthood. The penultimate moult, in which the nymph becomes a sub-imago, takes place at the water surface.

empty case of sub-imago

Mayflies are the only insects that have a sub-imago stage. The sub-imago (dun) resembles the adult insect in all but colour. The wings are non-transparent, and all colours are muted in comparison with the adult insect. The tail filaments are short, and the genitalia are not fully developed. A mayfly in the sub-imago stage does not feed. The sub-imago can fly, though not very well, being heavy with a gut full of water. After yet another moult, the light and elegant adult mayfly emerges. Empty sub-imago cases can often be spotted on plants in clumps of reeds. Mayflies are the only insects that moult after gaining wings.

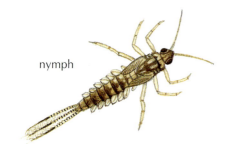

nymph

Pale Evening Dun
Procloeon bifidum

Nymph up to 10 mm. Sand-coloured with slightly darker patches on the upperside of the abdomen. It has three equally long tail filaments, with thin dark rings up to the middle and hairs a little way from the middle, and a broad dark band. Tail filaments are always held together. Occurs locally in sandy-bottomed rivers, June-August.

♂

nymph

Broadwing, Angler's Curse *Caenis horaria*

Nymph up to 10 mm. Grey or grey-brown. The second pair of gill lamellae have evolved into large plates, which cover the other gills like a skirt. Nymph swims by flexing its body through the water. Common on the bottom of ponds and lakes with abundant plant life, and can be found on sandy or stony bottoms. Several similar species, of which some can be found in streams and others on muddy lake bottoms.

Brachycercus harrisella

Nymph up to 11 mm. Grey-brown, with a small spine above each eye and a strong spine on the forehead. The second pair of gills have evolved into large plates, which cover the other gills. Rare. March-August. Adult flies only at night, July-September.

Many mayflies are caught by fish as they attempt to emerge from the final nymphal skin on the water's surface. For this reason, fishermen often use flies that resemble mayflies.

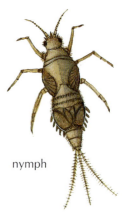

nymph

56

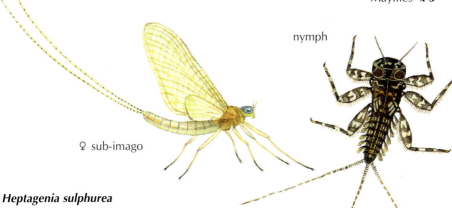

nymph

♀ sub-imago

Heptagenia sulphurea

Nymph up to 10 mm. Found especially on stones in fast-flowing streams and rivers, and on stones in the splash zone of lakes.
The adult mayfly has sulphur-yellow wings and flies June-September.

Heptagenia fuscogrisea

Nymph up to 15 mm. Flat head and body, with broad legs. Tail filaments are longer than body. Gill lamellae each have a bundle of gill filaments inside at the base. Feeds on algae etc. scraped off plants and stones. August-June. The adult flies May-June.

gill lamella of *Heptagenia sulphurea* and of *H. fuscogrisea*

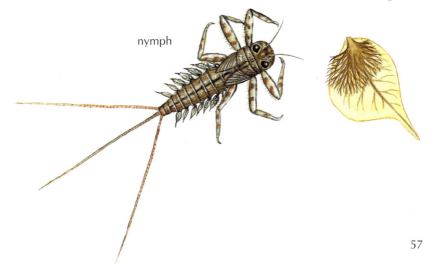

nymph

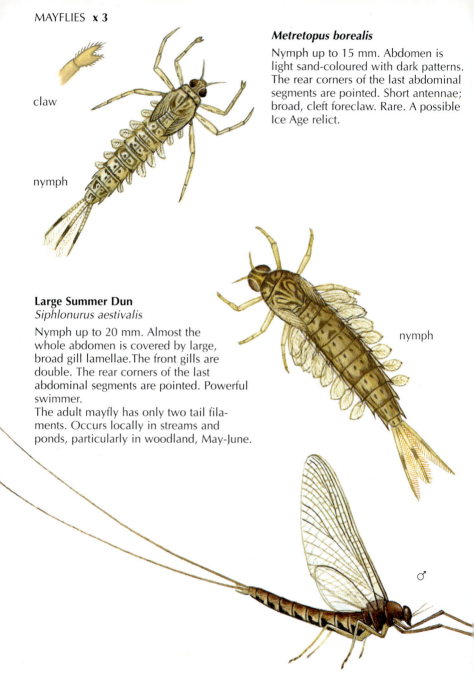

claw

nymph

Metretopus borealis

Nymph up to 15 mm. Abdomen is light sand-coloured with dark patterns. The rear corners of the last abdominal segments are pointed. Short antennae; broad, cleft foreclaw. Rare. A possible Ice Age relict.

Large Summer Dun
Siphlonurus aestivalis

Nymph up to 20 mm. Almost the whole abdomen is covered by large, broad gill lamellae. The front gills are double. The rear corners of the last abdominal segments are pointed. Powerful swimmer.
The adult mayfly has only two tail filaments. Occurs locally in streams and ponds, particularly in woodland, May-June.

nymph

♂

Mayfly *Ephemera danica*

Nymph up to 24 mm. Slender and cylindrical in its entire length. White-yellow, with dark triangular spots on the last abdominal segments. Very short tail filaments; mobile gills are feathery and folded in over the back. Short legs and powerful feet. Pair of mouthparts are shaped like tusks. Nymph lives buried in a U-shaped tube. Occurs locally all year round in fast- and moderately fast-flowing streams and rivers, particularly with sandy or gravelly bottoms.

The adult mayfly has very long antennae and three very long tail filaments. Wings are dark, but transparent, and abdomen is white with brown-black spots. Wingspan approx. 40 mm. Flies May-June.

A similar species, **E. vulgata**, is found buried in tunnels locally on sandy bottoms near the shores of clean lakes and in oxbow lakes. The adult Mayfly has shiny brown wings.

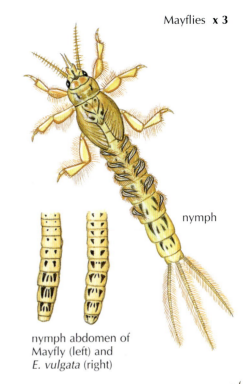

nymph

nymph abdomen of Mayfly (left) and *E. vulgata* (right)

Mayflies usually mate in the air after an elegant and characteristic mating flight (dance). The males die after mating. The females of some species lay their eggs by dipping their abdominal tip into the water as they fly.

STONEFLIES

Stoneflies have two long slender antennae, two long tail filaments and two pairs of narrow, glossy wings of almost equal size, which lie flat or rolled around the abdomen. They run well but fly badly, flapping with their abdomen hanging down. They fly only in good weather, in early morning or late evening. The female flies low over the water to lay her eggs singly or in clutches, usually just under the water surface. Stoneflies undergo partial metamorphosis, and the nymphs live primarily in streams. They have powerful legs with claws, long antennae and two long tail filaments and crawl around on the stream bottom, unable to swim. They take in oxygen through the skin, and gills, where present, are located on the prothorax, at the throat, or abdominal tip (not on sides of abdomen as in mayflies). Some feed on fallen leaves, while others are predators.

Taeniopteryx nebulosa

Nymph up to 15 mm. Brown-black with very long antennae and tail filaments. It has gills at the base of legs and spines on the upperside of the first 7 abdominal segments. Nymph hides in vegetation in slow muddy streams or rivers. July-April.
The adult is seen February-April, flying only in sunshine.

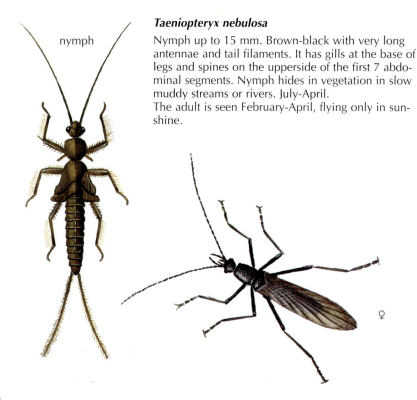

nymph

♀

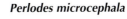

Perlodes microcephala

Nymph up to 25 mm. Strong; upper-side grey-brown with light markings and pale yellow on underside. Femur and tibia have a dense edging of hair on the back. First to fourth abdominal segments are divided into a back plate and a belly plate. Predator. Rare. September-April.

The adult male has short, unusable wings. This genus is usually in upland rivers.

nymph

Many species of stonefly are found in streams running through woodland or where there are trees along the banks. They feed on plants or are predators. Many adult stoneflies feed on lichen on trees, but some do not feed at all, just like mayflies.

STONEFLIES **x 3**

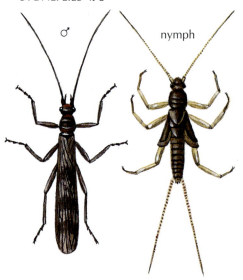

♂

nymph

nymph abdominal plate x 6

Brachyptera risi

Nymph up to 11 mm. Brown to brown-black, with long, fairly thick antennae and tail filaments. On the underside of the abdominal tip is a rhomboid plate. Nymphs often curl up if disturbed. Occurs locally in small fast-flowing streams, November-May.
Adult stonefly is seen April-June.

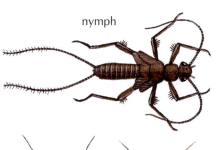

nymph

Nemurella picteti

Nymph up to 10 mm. Dark brown. Long, curving antennae and tail filaments; femur has a row of tough bristles on the upperside. Common all year round in rivers, streams and particularly in springs where the current is slow.

nymph

Protonemura meyeri

Nymph up to 10mm. Brown with long antennae and tail filaments, and three sausage-shaped gills on each side of the underside of the thorax. Occurs locally in fast-flowing springs, streams and rivers with stony and gravelly bottoms, August-June.
Adult stonefly is seen April-May.

Isoperla sp.

Nymph up to 18 mm. Olive-green to grey-brown
with light markings on head and body. Long hair
fringes on the rear side of femur and tibia. First two
abdominal segments are divided into a back plate
and a belly plate. Predator. Occurs locally in streams
and rivers, and some lakes. November-July.
Adult (Yellow Sally) stonefly is seen April-June.

nymph

Amphinemura standfussi

Nymph up to 8 mm. Brown, often dirty, with particles
between leg and body bristles. Antennae and tail
filaments are long, and it has two pairs of bushy gill
bundles on the underside of the thorax. Primarily
found in woodland in fairly fast-flowing springs and
streams with stony or gravelly bottoms, March-
September. Like *Protonemura*, this genus has bunches
of neck gills. Adult stonefly seen May-October. A
similar species, **A. sulcicollis,** prefers large streams
and rivers.

nymph

Nemoura cinerea

Nymph up to 10mm. Dull, densely
hairy, brown to dark brown, no gills.
Feeds on algae, and can be found in
all kinds of water under stones, tree
roots, among leaves etc. all year round
except August.
Adult stoneflies are seen April-October.
N. avicularis is only found in fast-
flowing streams and rivers and under
stones in the splash zone of lakes.

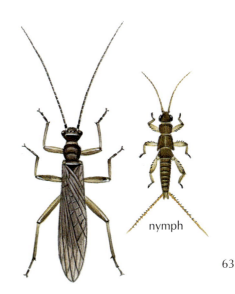

nymph

63

nymph

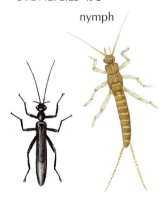

Leuctra sp.

Nymph up to 11 mm. Yellow to light brown, slender and worm-shaped, with long abdomen and powerful hind legs. The first abdominal segments are divided into a back plate and a belly plate. Found locally in fairly fast-flowing springs, woodland streams and rivers, often on stones or submerged pieces of wood, March-September.

Adults have their wings wrapped around their bodies, have very short tail filaments, and are seen April-October. Known as needle or willow flies.

abdomen of nymph x 6

Capnia bifrons

Nymph up to 11 mm. Brown-black, slender and worm-like. All abdominal segments are divided into a back plate and a belly plate. Not very common, but usually found in small streams that dry out in summer, particularly in deciduous woodland, September-March. In Britain this genus is found mainly in stony streams in the north and west.

The adult male stonefly, which is almost wingless, may be active as early as January-March, even on snow.

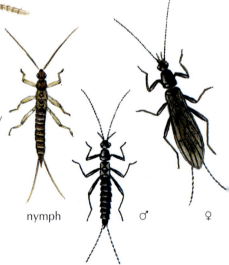

nymph　　　♂　　　♀

The nymphs of some of the stoneflies that live on stones in fast-flowing water are subjected to a constant bombardment of grains of sand of varying sizes. These nymphs, therefore, cannot be thin-skinned like other stonefly nymphs, with cutaneous respiration, but instead have thick skins, and breathe by means of gills.

Adult stoneflies fly so poorly that they tend to run away rather than fly when an attempt is made to catch them. When they do take to the air, they often fly in a straight line, as they are almost unable to navigate in the air.

Parasitic wasps and digger wasps

Parasitic wasps have a wasp-waist, and often long and extremely flexible antennae; the female has an ovipositor. The larvae live as parasites on or in arthropods.

A distinctive feature of digger wasps (or sand wasps) is the shape of the abdomen, which is slender at the front and rather bulbous towards the rear. They have a poisonous sting. The larvae feed on paralysed prey.

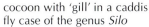
cocoon with 'gill' in a caddis fly case of the genus *Silo*

Agriotypus armatus

5-8 mm. This parasitic wasp has a shiny black thorax with a long, curved spine. Dark shaded wings. Adult wasp flies April-May. Female swims down to the bottom of a stream, using her wings, to lay eggs in case-bearing caddis fly larvae, particularly of the genera *Silo* and *Goera*. The larva waits until the caddis fly larva is almost fully developed and is about to close its case, then the parasitic wasp larva eats it, grows quickly and pupates in a cocoon spun inside the case. The cocoon has a very tough and slightly twisted brown band up to 25 mm long sticking out between the walls of the case and the door stone, as a kind of gill. The pupa overwinters. Occurs locally in stony-bottomed springs, streams and rivers.

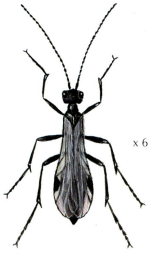

x 6

Trypoxylon figulus

8-12 mm, shiny black, slender and active digger wasp, with a narrow waist. Larvae found in reeds, which are divided up into small cells and closed with a clay plug at the entrance. They feed on small spiders, which the digger wasps have paralysed with their poison. Common in thatched roofs and in many washed-up or cut reeds on lakeshores, May-September.

FLIES, MIDGES AND MOSQUITOES

True-flies, order Diptera, have only one pair of wings. Their hind wings are reduced to small pin-like halteres, which help to stabilise their flight. Diptera include typical flies (such as hover-flies and house-flies), soldier-flies and horse-flies, as well as midges and mosquitoes. Midges and mosquitoes have long antennae, often longer than the head and thorax. More typical flies mostly have antennae that are shorter than the thorax. Dipteran larvae have no legs, though some species do have fleshy protuberances similar to the prolegs of a caterpillar.

Soldier-flies

Soldier-flies range from 3-18 mm in size. Their mesothorax is covered by a plate called the scutellum, often with one or more pairs of backward-pointing spines. The halteres are often coloured, and the abdomen is generally broad and flat. They are primarily seen on hot, sunny days, hovering around bushes and other plants, especially flowers of umbellifers. They feed on plant sap, nectar and pollen. They lay their eggs on plants, and the larvae make their way to water. Most larvae live in water or mud. They are more or less flattened, with thick, leathery, hardened skin and a highly inflexible, well-developed head. The rearmost body segment ends in a breathing tube with a crown of long hairs around the tip, which takes an air bubble with it when the larva goes under the water's surface. They feed largely on algae and detritus, though some are predators. Pupation takes place on land, in the last larval skin, which hardens into a puparium.

♀

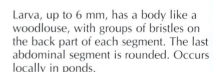

larva x 6

Beris vallata

5-6.5 mm. Black thorax; yellow abdomen. Female's wings are yellowish; male's are dark brown. It is not particularly active and is somewhat shy. Seen June-August.

Larva, up to 6 mm, has a body like a woodlouse, with groups of bristles on the back part of each segment. The last abdominal segment is rounded. Occurs locally in ponds.

Stratiomys furcata

13-18 mm. Shiny black abdomen with a yellow tip and yellow side-spots on the upperside. Light brownish wings laid parallel over the abdomen at rest. Seen May-August. Larva, up to 60 mm, is elongated, with its broadest point near the middle, and very narrow at the rear, particularly the last segment, which has a crown of long, feathery hairs around the breathing hole. Occurs locally in ponds and bogs. It can tolerate long periods of drought and can live in saline water.

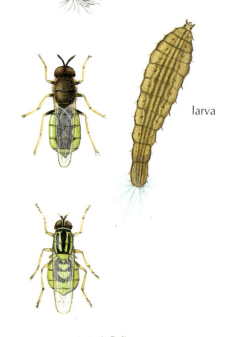

larva

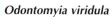

Odontomyia viridula

6-8 mm. Black thorax, with dense yellow hair. Broad, flat abdomen, light green or yellow, with black central stripe. Clear wings; yellow legs. Common in meadows and bogs, June-August.
Larva is elongated, but the last segment is shorter and broader than in *Stratiomys*. Occurs locally in ponds and lakes and can live in saline water.

larva

Oxycera trilineata

5-7 mm. Yellow or green thorax, with three broad black stripes. Yellow or green abdomen has black markings. Clear wings. Seen June-August.
Larva is oval and elongated. The last segment is longer than broad, rounded at the back, and with a crown of feathery hairs around the breathing hole. Occurs locally among moss on stones in springs and streams, but also lives in ditches and ponds.

larva x 6

♀

Snipe-flies

Snipe-flies generally have a slender abdomen and long, slender legs. Their antennae have three segments, the outermost being divided into two long branches. The female has widely-separated eyes and a pointed abdomen ending in an ovipositor. The male's eyes are closer together, and its abdomen is shorter.

larva

Atherix ibis

8.5-10 mm. Brown-spotted wings. Male has a brown-black thorax with two lighter grey longitudinal stripes. Yellow-brown abdomen with black patches on the top and along the sides. Female's abdomen is grey with black transverse bands. It is a predator, attacking small flies in particular. Often rests on tree trunks with its head downwards. May-July.

Larva, up to 20 mm, is cylindrical and pointed at the front end. Abdomen has curved, flexible spines, one pair of pro-legs under each segment, and a pair of long, pointed tracheal gills at the rear end. Found only on stony bottoms in moderately fast-flowing streams and rivers. It overwinters as a larva.

When the females lay eggs, they gather like small swarms of bees under bridges or on branches over streams. The eggs are held together by a sticky mass, and this clump may reach the size of a large grapefruit. The females die, but remain clustered with the egg mass. The larvae feed on them and on the mass, until they fall into the water, where they live as predators.

individual eggs and clump of dead females

Hover-flies

These agile insects are usually to be seen hovering in front of flowers, particularly daisies and umbellifers, or resting on flowers to suck nectar, especially on sunny days in summer and autumn. The head is large, with well-developed eyes and short antennae; the abdomen is usually broad and flat with black and yellow markings. The larvae are either free-living aphid-eaters, or live in a variety of habitats, including water, mud and dung.

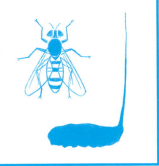

Rat-tailed maggot is the common name for certain larvae that have a fat, round body, and an extending, flexible breathing tube up to 5 cm long. Rat-tailed maggots lie buried at the bottom; they feed on organic matter and can live in the most polluted watercourses, in ditches, ponds and drains. Their natural habitat is small pools, such as holes in trees.

Drone-fly
Eristalis tenax

14-16 mm. Abdomen has brown patches and transverse bands. Feeds on pollen and nectar from flowers, and flies all year round in warm, sunny weather, but primarily in August-September. Overwinters as adult in hollow trees, cellars, out-houses etc. It resembles a honeybee drone, hence its name.

Larva, up to 20 mm, is whitish and sausage-shaped, with 7 pairs of hooked prolegs. The breathing tube can be as much as several times longer than the body, and has 8 long feathered hairs at the tip. Because of its long breathing tube the larva is called a rat-tailed maggot; this adaptation allows it to breathe at the surface and live in badly polluted, oxygen-deficient water. Several similar species.

larva

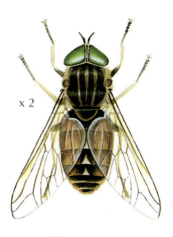

x 2

Horse-flies

These are large flies with big, beautifully-coloured eyes, short thick antennae, and clear or spotted wings. With a top speed of 30-50 km/h, horse-flies are among the fastest flying insects. The male feeds on nectar from flowers, while the female sucks blood from large animals, including humans. Their eggs are laid in clusters on plants and stones in damp locations. The larvae, which are cylindrical, and pointed at both ends, make their way to water. They are whitish, brownish or greenish, with longitudinal stripes. At the front of each abdominal segment are four pairs of bulges, 1 pair on the upperside and at the sides, and two on the underside. The head can be pulled into the body; the abdominal tip has a breathing tube. Most are predators, sucking their prey dry. They live in mud along the edges of puddles, ponds and lakes, or in damp soil.

Tabanus bovinus

18-23 mm, clear wings and transverse stripes and brown patches on abdomen. Especially common in open woodland and along paths and tracks. Flies May-August. Audible in flight. Larva, up to 30 mm, has no stripes, unlike the larva of Chrysops relictus. Found in damp earth; feeds primarily on beetle larvae.
A similar, but larger, species, **T. sudeticus**, 19-25 mm, sucks blood primarily from horses.

Chrysops relictus

8-12 mm, with a yellow-spotted body and brown patches on the wings, which are held in a triangle at rest. Very common near water, June-August, and clearly audible in flight. Larva, up to 14 mm, is striped all over, including the upperside of the thoracic segments. Predator. Found on shores of clean lakes, but also in tufts of moss in springs; feeds on algae and detritus.

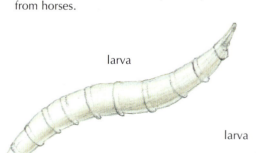

larva

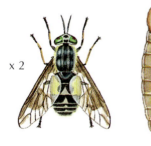

x 2

larva

pupa seen from above

The female pesters large animals and humans, cutting a triangular hole in the skin with razor-sharp mouth-parts to suck blood. The bite is painful, causing large swellings and allergic reactions in some humans. They tend not to bite in enclosed spaces, as when trapped in a car.

Although they have large eyes, they are actually not very quick at moving away, so they are easy to kill when they settle to bite and suck blood.

x 2

Cleg-fly (Cleg)
Haematopota pluvialis

8-13 mm, slender, with soot-coloured wings, held close over the abdomen at rest. Especially common near water and can be a nuisance in damp weather. Flies June-August. Silent in flight.
Larva closely resembles that of *Tabanus bovinus*, but is half the size and has a shorter breathing tube.

Psilopa nitidula

A shore-fly, 2-3 mm, small and plump, shiny black with red eyes; transparent wings have two small gaps at front edges (costal breaks).
Larva, up to 4 mm, has a dark head and prothorax, and has 8 pairs of hooked prolegs under the abdomen, of which the last pair is quite large and covered in bristles. The rear end is drawn out in a long breathing tube divided in two. Feeds on algae and detritus and occurs in shallow water among plants in ponds and lakes. Some species are common in brackish water and salt water.

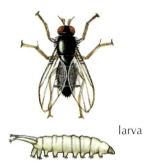

larva

Ephydra riparia

A shore-fly. Up to 5 mm. Dark, brownish or black. Occasionally found swarming in huge numbers over water in salt marshes or over pools near the sea.
Larva, up to 6 mm, is greenish, has 8 pairs of prolegs, is pointed at both front and rear ends and has a long, forked breathing tube. Feeds on single-celled animals and algae. Pupates clinging tightly to a straw.

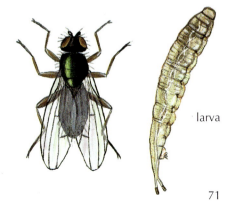

larva

Hydromyza livens

6-8 mm. A greenish or blue-grey dung-fly, very hairy. Head has red-yellow forehead.
Larva is limbless, but has bulges surrounding the spiracles on the abdominal tip. It mines the stems and leaves of yellow water-lilies, forming U-shaped tunnels from the centre of the leaves. Occurs locally in ponds and lakes.

larva

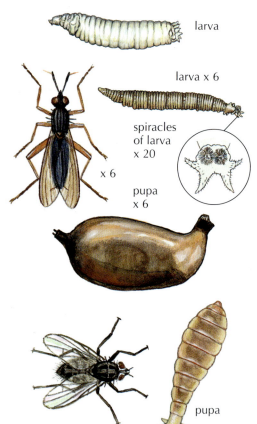

larva x 6

spiracles
of larva
x 20

x 6

pupa
x 6

Sepedon sp.

4-5 mm, grey-black, with relatively long antennae and long, powerful legs. Dark wings, with light patches, lying flat over the abdomen at rest.
Larvae, up to 6 mm, are limbless, and have two spiracles at the rear end, surrounded by four long bulges. Most feed on freshwater snails and pupate in their shells. A few feed on bivalves. Particularly common in ponds with abundant plant life, hanging onto the surface film by means of the hairy fringes around its spiracles.

Limnophora sp.

A member of the house-fly family. Very hairy; long, dark abdomen, occasionally metallic blue or green. Overwinters as both adult and larva.
Grub-like larva, up to 16 mm, is white to yellowish, ringed, with a pair each of pseudo-legs and spiracles on the last abdominal segment. A predator, feeding primarily on worms and the larvae of non-biting midges and other flies. Common; found May-August, especially on moss in small puddles near lakes, streams and waterfalls.
Pupation takes place in the last larval skin, which hardens to become a fat, barrel-shaped puparium with a clear mosaic structure.

pupa

larva

Dance-flies

Dance-flies (empids) are 1.5-14 mm long, with slender legs, short antennae and large eyes. They have a long and slender abdomen, curved up at the rear in the male. They dance in swarms, often in their thousands, above water or nearby. The larvae of most species live on damp ground by riverbanks and lakeshores. Some are found on moss and algae on stones in clean, running water. They are all predators.

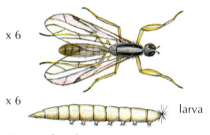

x 6

x 6

larva

Hemerodromia sp.

4-5 mm. Elongated, with large, clear, iridescent wings and powerful forelegs. Larva has a long, pointed head. Abdomen has 7 pairs of strong, bristly pseudo-legs, and its rear end has a crown of long hairs. Pupa has long, bristle-like protuberances. Common among moss and algae on stones in streams and rivers.

Clinocera sp.

Long larva with bristly pseudo-legs under the abdomen. Rear pair are largest. Rear end has four bristly appendages. Common in streams and rivers.

larva x 6

Long-legged Flies

Long-legged flies are slender, 2-10 mm long, with long legs, often metallic green or blue. The wings, with only one cross-vein, are held flat over the body at rest. When the fly is still, the head and thorax are raised up high. The male has a powerful sex organ, held bent in under its abdomen. Many species have distinctly ornamented foot segments, which the male waves in front of the female before mating. They are predators, feeding on small insects and worms, and can be spotted running around on mud, aquatic plants, and even on the water surface.
The larvae are also predators, living in damp earth; they are found primarily at the edges of ponds and lakes.

Dolichopus ungulatus

5.5-6.5 mm. Shiny green. Common by ponds and small lakes in summer, especially in woodland. They feed primarily on mosquitoes, which they suck dry.
Larva has two pairs of protuberances at the rear end. It also has 7 hoop-shaped rings around its body.

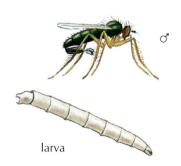

♂

larva

Crane-flies

Crane-flies (also known as daddy-long-legs) have a long abdomen, two wings and legs that are often twice the length of their body. The hind wings have been modified into small halteres to stabilise flight. The adults eat almost nothing. Some are large, but most are small. They can be seen dancing in swarms like non-biting midges. The worm-like larvae, often with tail appendages around the breathing holes, are able to pull their head partially or fully into their body. Many live in damp earth, rotten tree stumps etc. Some are found in water, where they feed on plant roots or dead organic matter, while others are predators. They often come up onto land to pupate in damp earth above the water line.

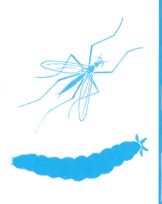

x 1

Tipula maxima

Wing length 27-30 mm. Largest British fly. Wings have large, dark, triangular patches, and are held almost at right angles to the body at rest. Red-brown abdomen with dark longitudinal stripes. Common May-August.
Larva, up to 60 mm, is dark grey, brown or brown-green and has no pro-legs. Rear end has 6 appendages surrounding the breathing holes. Common in moss and mud in shallow water in springs and streams, particularly in woodland, where it feeds on rotting leaves from deciduous trees.

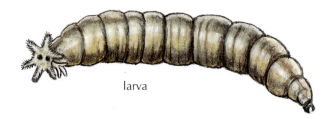

larva

Phalacrocera replicata

Wing length 12-14 mm. Wings held together over abdomen at rest. Abdomen is red-brown with a dark dorsal stripe and dark side stripes. Common; seen primarily in the evening.
Larva, up to 30 mm, is brown or green with narrow light rings and rows of long filaments on the body, with slightly shorter tracheal gills on the sides and belly. Long point at the rear end. Found only among sphagnum moss in ponds and small lakes. Pupa hangs below the water surface, floating horizontally.
A similar species, *Triogma* sp., whose larvae have shorter and fatter tracheal gills and bristles, is found in the same places and in springs.

x 1

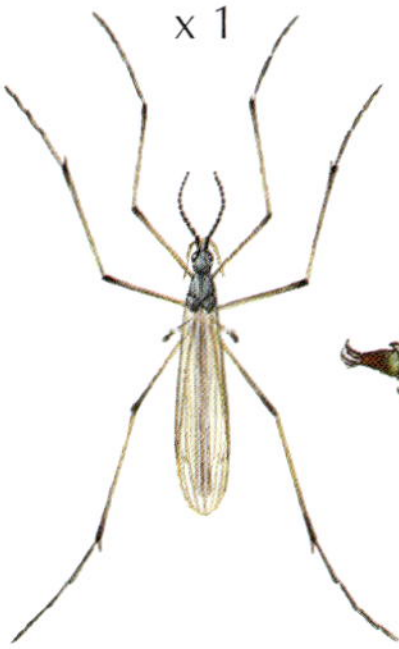

pupa

larva

Pedicia rivosa

Wing length 18-25 mm. Wings are clear, with a brown front edge and a V-shaped mark in the centre. Slate-grey abdomen has broad, dark grey central stripe and is edged with dark brown.
Larva, up to 40 mm, is whitish, with four pairs of prolegs and short branched tail notches. It is a predator, feeding primarily on the larvae of non-biting midges. Occurs locally in springs, woodland streams and ditches.

x 1

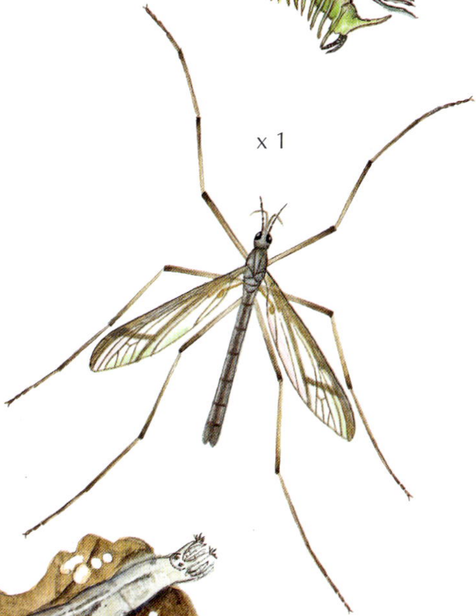

larva

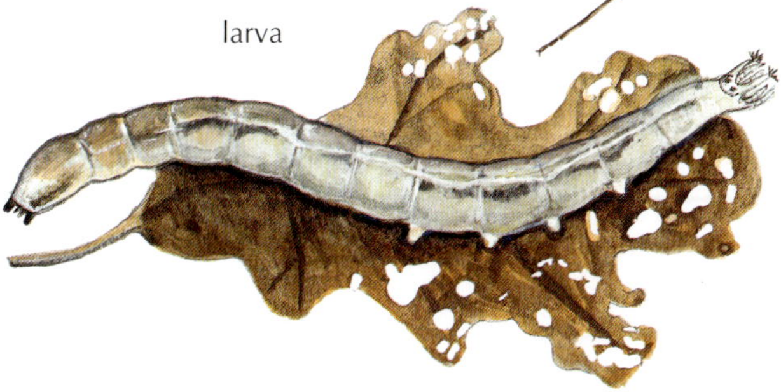

larva

larva

Pseudolimnophila sp.

Larva 14-16 mm. Whitish or yellow; rear segments darker. Tail appendages are dark on the upperside and have long, pale-yellow hair along the sides. Feeds on detritus. Very common in muddy bottoms by riverbanks.

Dicranota sp.

Larva, up to 30 mm, is greenish, with five pairs of prolegs and two long bristly appendages on the abdominal tip. A predator, feeding on small worms. Common on sandy bottoms in springs, streams and rivers.

Crane-flies can lose one or more legs without apparent inconvenience. A kicking leg may distract a predator, allowing the crane-fly to escape further pursuit.

Many crane-fly species can rapidly vibrate their body by moving their legs. This makes them less visible, allowing them to escape predators.

abdomen ♂   abdomen ♀

Males have a flat, blunt tip to abdomen. Females have a pointed abdomen, and fly in a hopping manner over soil or water, where they lay their eggs.

Phantom crane-flies

Phantom crane-flies are shiny black, slender, medium-sized flies, measuring 8-10 mm. They resemble crane-flies, but have long antennae and long, often striped legs, with large tibial spurs. They have a long abdomen and narrow, distinctly-veined wings. The larvae have one short or long telescopic breathing tube. They are found partially buried in shallow water in ponds, lakes and streams, where they feed on detritus. The pupae have two breathing tubes, one short and one longer than the body. At the front of the body the wing outlines are distinctly visible, as are the leg outlines on the underside which are longer and lie parallel.

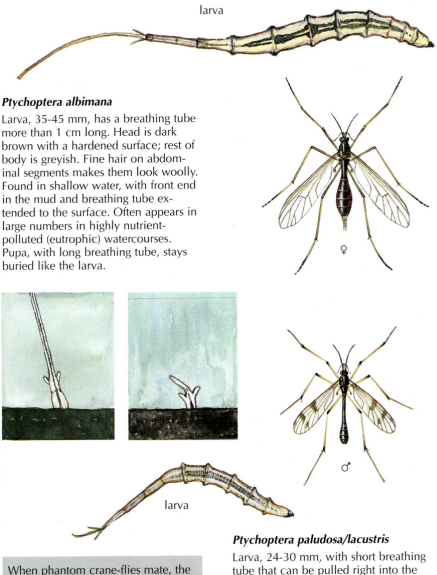

larva

Ptychoptera albimana

Larva, 35-45 mm, has a breathing tube more than 1 cm long. Head is dark brown with a hardened surface; rest of body is greyish. Fine hair on abdominal segments makes them look woolly. Found in shallow water, with front end in the mud and breathing tube extended to the surface. Often appears in large numbers in highly nutrient-polluted (eutrophic) watercourses. Pupa, with long breathing tube, stays buried like the larva.

♀

♂

larva

When phantom crane-flies mate, the male and female are coupled together at the rear end, and may fly in tandem, with the female leading.

Ptychoptera paludosa/lacustris

Larva, 24-30 mm, with short breathing tube that can be pulled right into the abdomen. Yellow-brown head with light patches. Common in shallow water in ditches and streams, especially in woodland.

Non-biting Midges

Non-biting midges are 2-12 mm long. They have reduced mouth parts and cannot bite. Their body is black or grey, and their wings do not extend beyond the abdominal tip. The larger species rest with their forelegs raised high above their head. The males (plumed gnats) have very feathery antennae and dance in large swarms. Any female ready to mate that flies into the swarm is caught immediately. The swarms, which can resemble small clouds, may be seen almost anywhere in still weather, not only above water.

The larvae, up to 30 mm, are colourless, red or green. They breathe through the skin and are found in all kinds of water. They are slender, resembling worms, but have a distinct head, and one pair of prolegs on the first thoracic segment and one pair on the last abdominal segment. The rear end may also have worm-like appendages or bristles. They may be free-moving or remain fixed in one place. They feed on detritus and plankton, although some are predatory, commensal or parasitic, or they may mine leaves of aquatic plants.

These larvae play a large part in the conversion of material in aquatic environments. They are a food source for many predatory insects and larger predators, e.g. eels and other deep water fish, and they can be found in concentrations up to 50,000 per m^2 on the bottom.

Prodiamesa olivacea

Larva is pale, has long bristles under the head and eyes that are positioned obliquely over each other. It is very common in streams, where it feeds on detritus and bacteria; it can tolerate quite high levels of pollution and turbidity.

head of larva
x 20

Orthocladius sp.

Green larva has short antennae on a base. Its two eyes are located one right behind the other and may be almost fused together. Lives in unpolluted watercourses.

larva seen from above
and from the side x 6

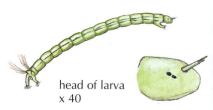

head of larva
x 40

Chironomus anthracinus

Swarms in large numbers in May, at about the time when beech trees come into leaf.

Red larva has two eyes, one above the other. Found in conical silk-lined tube in cold, oxygen-deficient parts of lakes. Feeds on detritus in upper layers of lake-bed sediments. The air-filled pupa sits in its tube, rising to the surface as an air bubble in the evening. It has rows of hairs on its head, which push through the surface film, the pupal case then splits, after which the adult insect breaks out. The entire sequence takes place between 7pm and 1am, lasting approx. 35 seconds. Common on the beds of lakes in northern Europe.

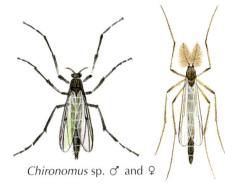

Chironomus sp. ♂ and ♀

The blood of the red larvae of non-biting midges contains oxygen-binding haemoglobin. They are therefore able to live in highly polluted or oxygen-deficient water, where they may be found in vast numbers.

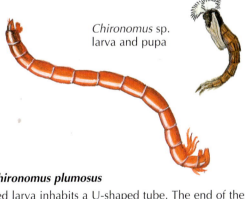

Chironomus sp. larva and pupa

Chironomus plumosus

Red larva inhabits a U-shaped tube. The end of these tubes stick out from the mud floor like chimneys. Feeds on fallen detritus, algae and bacteria, which it catches in a net within the tube, gnaws on the tube's sticky inside, or stretches its front end out to eat from the lakebed surface. Very common in shallow, nutrient-rich lakes, but also found towards the edges of deeper lakes.

79

The larvae of some non-biting midges are often found living in mayfly nymph tubes, in black-fly pupal cases and in snail shells. Occasionally the head of a red non-biting midge larva can be seen sticking out of a river snail's shell. Some larvae simply use the snail for protection and transport, without doing it any harm. Others feed on the snail, devouring it slowly. The larvae subsequently pupate inside the snail shell.

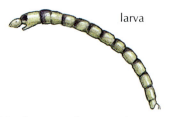

larva

Metriocnemus hygropetricus

Larva is greenish yellow, with a broad violet ring on each segment. Feeds on the surface of aquatic plants, close to the water surface, in spring. Fairly common.

Tanytarsus sp.

Larva, up to 6 mm, is greenish or reddish, with long antennae. The two eyes are located one above the other. It is common in ponds on heathland or dunes. Several similar species live in running water and in lakes, where they may form dense layers covering stones and aquatic plants.

Rheotanytarsus sp.

Larva green, with long antennae. It constructs shelters from mud particles and its own droppings, fixing 1-5 longitudinal ribs on the outside that protrude past the opening. Between the ribs it spins a coarse web of sticky silk threads to catch algae and small particles. The larva eats what it requires, using the rest to extend its tube. Occurs locally on stones and aquatic plants in large, moderately fast-flowing streams.

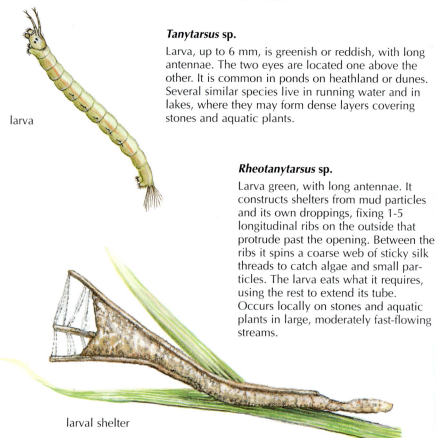

larva

larval shelter

egg mass of non-biting midge

Procladius sp.

6-7 mm. Clear wings with brown patches, shorter than body. Body brown, with light transverse bands. Forms swarms on shores of ponds and lakes.

Larva, up to 15 mm, is greenish and transparent, with a long, divided pro-leg with hooks at the front. Long, slender head and long antennae, which can be pulled into the body. Does not live in a tube, but is a highly mobile predator. It is very fast and catches small crustaceans, worms and mosquito larvae in reed thickets at the bottom of ponds and lakes, and is also found in deep water in lakes. Very common.

x 3

larva

swarm of non-biting midges by an alder tree

Phantom midges

Phantom midges are small, pale, brownish flies, seen in large swarms over lakes and ponds through-out most of the year. Their wings are laid flat over the abdomen at rest. The adults do not bite. Eggs are laid surrounded by jelly in round, flat clusters on the water surface. The larvae are predators, lying horizontally in the water and feeding mainly on small crustaceans. They have hinged antennae, which can be snapped together like claws, and their three thoracic segments are fused together and are broader than the abdomen. On the underside of the last abdominal segment is a fan of bristles. The larvae and pupae live floating in water.

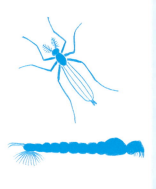

Chaoborus sp.

6-7 mm. Female's wings extend as far as abdominal tip. Male has shorter wings and bushy antennae. The larva (phantom larva) is transparent, up to 12 mm, does not come up to the surface to breathe, but uses cutaneous respiration. The tracheal system has been modified into two pairs of curved swim bladders, functioning as hydrostatic organs to stabilise the larva in the water. It may remain buried at the bottom by day, but floats in the water at night. The pupa, with prothorax and head fused together, is mobile and has two swimming plates at the abdominal tip. After 3-4 days it drifts up to the surface, where metamorphosis takes place. Found in large numbers, particularly in lakes, but also in ponds, occasionally in quite deep water.

egg mass

larva

pupa

Mochlonyx culiciformis

5-6 mm. Resembles *Chaoborus*, but is smaller. Larva, up to 8 mm, is clear, slightly brown, with air bladders in the prothorax. It has a breathing tube at the rear end, but only occasionally takes in air at the surface. Found mostly in small ponds.

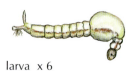

larva x 6

Meniscus midges

Meniscus midges are small non-biting flies. The body is normally brown, with quite large, broad wings, twice the length of the abdomen. They have long legs and antennae, which, unlike mosquitoes, are not bushy in the male. They are seen throughout most of the year near water.

The larvae are U-shaped and lie on stones and plants in streams or by the shores of ponds and lakes, with their head and abdomen dipping down under the surface film; they also move in a bendy fashion. They feed on bacteria and detritus filtered from the surface film. The pupa has two breathing tubes and two fused swimming plates on the abdominal tip, but no spines or bristles, and it lies curled up like a ball.

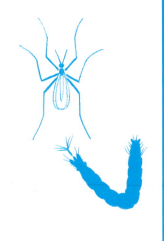

Dixa sp.

Larva, up to 8 mm, is greyish, rather flattened, with false legs under the first and second abdominal segments. It also has long bristles behind the head and at the abdominal tip. Always lies curled up like a U or a J. Primarily found on stones, branches, plants etc. in springs, but can also be found in fast-flowing streams and rivers. Pupa is approx. 3 mm long when curled up. A smaller species is found on the shores of ponds with abundant plant life.

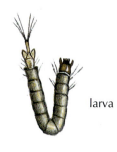

larva

Dixella sp.

4-5 mm. Resembles a small crane-fly or mosquito, but does not bite. Brown, slender body, long, thin legs, and large, broad, clear wings. Antennae are longer than thorax and are not bushy. Common near shores of ponds. Larva, up to 8 mm, is dark and rests on stones and aquatic plants right at the water surface like an inverted U, with its front and rear ends curved down into the water. Several similar species.

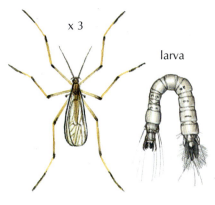

x 3

larva

Thaumalea testacea

larva

Green-brown larva, up to 15 mm, is long and thin, with a brown head and one pair of false legs under the prothorax and one pair of hairy spiracles on stalks at the sides.

It moves in a U-shape like meniscus midges and turns fast somersaults when disturbed. Quite rare, but found on stones, branches etc. in springs. Feeds on algae.

Mosquitoes

Mosquitoes have a long proboscis, long legs and clear wings, held flat over the abdomen at rest. They often rest with the hind legs raised. The male has bushy antennae, feeds on nectar and does not bite. The female bites and sucks blood in order to form eggs, which are laid singly or in batches. The larvae are long, with bristly bodies, and are primarily found in small pools and ponds. They pupate after 5-8 weeks. The pupae are very flexible, with a long tail and a large, spherical, fused head and thorax. They hang from the surface, the adult breaking out after 3-4 days.

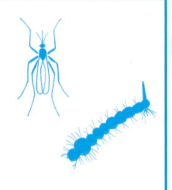

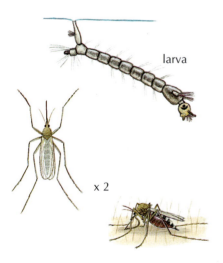

larva

x 2

Aedes sp.

7-8 mm. Adult rests with its body almost parallel to the surface. Palps are short. Eggs are laid edgewise close beside each other in clusters on the undersides of leaves etc. in dried-up puddles and small ponds; they overwinter. One generation a year. Larvae have a long breathing tubes with two breathing holes, and only one pair of bristle bundles or individual bristles. They hang head down from the water surface, feeding on small particles and may be found in puddles in woodland.

Several similar species; the larvae of some species are found in waterholes in meadows, whilst others live in brackish pools on salt marshes. Members of this genus often bite people.

Anopheles sp.

9-11 mm, more slender and more finely built than other mosquitoes, has longer legs, and rests with its body at an
oblique angle in relation to the surface
it is on. Wings are spotted, and palps
are same length as proboscis. Eggs are
laid in a star-shape or singly in small,
clean ponds with abundant plant life,
and in small pools in houses, stables
etc. 1-2 generations a year. Overwinters as adult. This genus transmits
malaria in some regions (especially in
the tropics).

Larvae, up to 9 mm, are green, lying
horizontally under the water's surface.
They feed on small single-celled algae,
bacteria and small particles, and
can turn over onto their backs and sweep
off anything edible on the surface.

One species, **A. plumbeus**, has unmarked wings. Its larva is found in
small woodland ponds, where it also
overwinters.

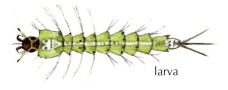

larva

Anopheles mosquitoes can transmit
malaria. The disease is caused by
single-celled organisms (protistans)
of the genus *Plasmodium*, living as
parasites in the blood. These live
in the mosquito, and their progeny
are transmitted to humans through
the saliva of infected mosquitoes,
where they attack human red
blood cells. These are picked up
by mosquitoes when they suck
human blood, and thus the cycle
repeats itself. Malaria kills over 1
million people a year in the
tropics.

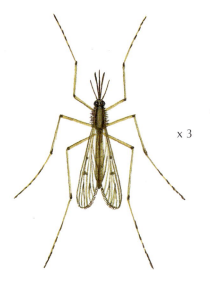

x 3

Midges and mosquitoes are particularly attracted to warmth. When
one bites, its saliva prevents the
blood from coagulating, and it is
this that makes the bite itch. The
swelling of the skin is due to the
body sending extra blood to the bite.

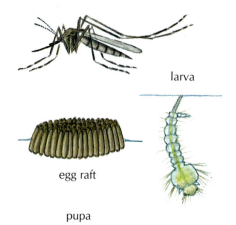

larva

egg raft

pupa

Culex pipiens

6-7 mm. Grey-brown, with a thin white band on each abdominal segment, and unmarked wings. Short palps. Rests almost parallel with the surface. Eggs are dark and elongated, and are laid closely together in rafts on the water surface.

Larvae, up to 9 mm, have several pairs of bristle bundles or individual bristles on their breathing tubes. They live in small pools, puddles and ponds. Several generations a year. Overwinters as adult. Also found indoors, but does not bite in winter. This species tends to bite birds rather than mammals.

Mosquitoes produce an audible hum when they fly. Their wings beat more than 300 times a second. They can fly quite fast, but do not fly very high.

The male hears using hairs on its antennae that act as kind of tuning fork. They are primarily listening for the buzzing sound of females.

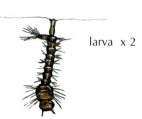

larva x 2

Culiseta annulata

9-11 mm. Large and dark, with spotted wings and with white rings on its legs and abdomen. Larva is not very sensitive to pollution and can live in small pools, gutters, and the like. Overwinters as adult indoors and has a very painful bite, even in winter.

Midges

Midges are small, greyish flies, slender and 1-3 mm long. They have a large, bulging thorax. Their wings, which can beat over a thousand times a second, usually have light-grey stripes or spots, and are laid flat over the abdomen at rest. The male has feathery antennae. The female has biting and sucking mouthparts, and feeds on blood from vertebrates and insects. Their eggs are laid in masses or in long strings, and are covered by a jelly-like substance. The larvae, which overwinter, can live in water, peat bogs, mud and damp earth, as well as in brackish water. They can feed on detritus and plants, or be predators or parasites on birds.

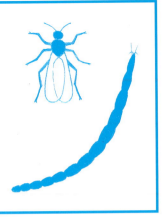

Heleinae

Larvae, up to 10 mm, are very slender, with small tail filaments. Predator. Common in all kinds of freshwater.

Biting (more strictly blood-sucking) midges can appear in huge swarms in summer, particularly at dusk in still weather. However, they also bite in hot, overcast weather in the daytime, and can make it unbearable out of doors.

In the tropics they transmit several life-threatening diseases. Adult midges rare–ly go further than a few hundred metres from the place where they were hatched, though they may be carried far away by the wind.

Egg mass and adult of midge

Midge larvae

Atrichopogon sp.

Larva, up to 3 mm, has downward-pointing head and long protuberances on its abdomen. Prothorax has protuberances resembling legs. Occurs locally on stones and moss in springs. Some feed on plants and detritus, others on algae, which they scrape off stones.

larva x 10

Black-flies

Black-flies are small, compact midges, 1.2-5.5 mm long, resembling small flies. Males are a dull black with silvery white patches; females are more grey-brown. Antennae and legs are short with silvery white rings. The thorax is short and bulging, and the wings are broad and powerful. The larva has adapted to life in running water and can be found in even the strongest current. Its three rear abdominal segments are swollen, making the larva resemble a small club. The back segment has a crown of hooks, with which the larva clings on to stones and plants. It moves like an inchworm, with a silken thread as a safety line. Its head has two large fans of sticky bristles, which it uses to filter algae and bacteria from the water. A few species are common in polluted and bacteria-laden water, and they can be found in very large numbers in such sites as reservoirs and downstream of fish-farms. The pupa, often found on stones and plants, lies fastened by abdominal hooks to a finely-woven pupal case shaped like a flattened cornet or slipper, with its point facing the current. Two branched silvery gills protrude from the opening. The names in brackets are the subgenera.

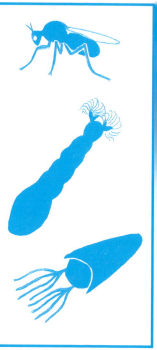

Black-fly sp.
adult and larva

Unlike midges, black-flies can fly several kilometres away from the place where they were hatched. Many female black-flies suck blood, particularly from mammals and birds, and in the tropics they can transmit parasites to humans, causing blindness. In Europe they may appear in such large numbers that they become intolerable for humans and animals, and mass attacks have been known to kill cattle and horses.

When a black-fly has settled to suck blood, it is rather hard to dislodge, making it easy to swat. Black-flies do not generally enter houses.

Simulium (Nevermannia) sp.

Head-shield yellow-brown or dark. Pupa, 3-4 mm, has 4-branched gill filaments up to 6 mm long. Pupal case is finely woven and has a long, straight horn and a pronounced ridge on the back. Common in springs, streams and rivers.

The fully-developed fly rises from the pupa to the surface in a small air bladder. When this bursts, the fly has to take to its wings as fast as possible. Many do not manage it and get eaten by fish.

pupa

Simulium (Wilhelmia) sp.

Pupa, 2-4.5 mm, has 1-2 mm long, thin-walled gills. Pupal case is finely woven with a rim. Can appear in large numbers, but only attacks cattle (especially the ears).

pupa

pupa

Simulium (Boopthora) erythrocephalum

Pupa, 2.2-3.5 mm, with 6-branched gill filaments up to 5 mm long. Pupal case is finely woven with a thin dorsal edge. Common in large rivers, particularly in outflows from lakes, and can be a local problem, feeding on blood of cattle.

Simulium (Odagmia) sp.

Larva 3.6-10 mm. Greyish or greenish with dark transverse bands. Head shield yellowish, light or dark brown. Pupa, 2-4 mm, has 8-branched gill filaments 2-3 mm long. Pupal case is finely woven with a pronounced dorsal ridge. The most widespread subgenus of black-fly.

pupa

Pericoma sp.

larva

4-5 mm, very hairy, with brown-spotted wings.
Larva, up to 8 mm, is flat and black, with long bristles on the back of each segment. Has four bristly appendages on the abdomen. Some species only live in clean water in fast-flowing springs and streams, and are found under tufts of moss, carpets of leaves etc.

Owl-midges

Owl-midges are small and very hairy. Their wings, which are also hairy, with brown spots and numerous long veins, are held partially unfolded or roofwise over the body at rest. Their flight is short and jumpy. They are often found in large numbers, at breeding site. The larvae take in air through their rear end, and they can therefore be seen close to or at the water surface.

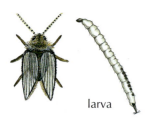

Psychoda sp.

2-3 mm, plain brown, with clear, overlapping wings. Often seen on aquatic plants.
Larva, up to 5mm, is whitish with short dorsal bristles on all segments. Dark head and abdominal tip. Lives in sewage works, waste pipes, traps, among rotten leaves, in dung, decayed snails etc. Larval period is 1-3 weeks.

larva

APHIDS

Aphids are 0.5-7 mm long, often pear-shaped, and vary in colour. Some species live in dense colonies on their host plants. Some with and some without transparent wings, held roofwise over the body at rest. They have a proboscis and two tubes (cornicles) on their back, or sometimes just pores.

Hyalopterus pruni

2-3 mm, elongated, pale green or brownish red and mealy. Lives in dense colonies on reeds.

Citadella viridis

A leafhopper. Female 8-9 mm, male 6-7 mm. Yellow legs; powerful, hairy jumping legs. Female's elytra are green, male's are bluish green, bluish black, or sometimes green. Feeds on sap, which it sucks through a short proboscis. Common on rushes, June-September.

Slender Groundhopper *Tetrix subulata*

9-12 mm. A groundhopper with greyish-brown body. The prothorax extends like a long thorn, and juts out over the abdominal tip. Will fly away if disturbed, and can run on water and dive down and swim by kicking its rear legs. The air trapped beneath its wings keeps it afloat. It cannot sing, and feeds on plants. Overwinters as nymph. Common on marshy meadows with short grass on the banks of lakes and rivers, March-June and September-October. In Britain mainly southern.

Large Marsh Grasshopper
Stethophyma grossum

21-25 mm. A grasshopper with olive-green body. The rear thighs are red on the inside, the knees are black, and the tibiae are bright yellow with black spines. Active in sunny weather and quick to fly up if disturbed. Males can fly 10 m, while the heavier, clumsier females fly only a short distance and try to hide among plants.

Feeds on plants. Its song is a series of short ticking phrases of 2-3 clicks per second. Lays eggs in autumn by grass roots in tussocks, and overwinters as nymph.
Found mainly on acid bogs in Ireland and western Britain.

Water bugs

Water bugs have stinging or sucking mouthparts, forming a proboscis. Their elytra are leathery at the front and membranous at the back. They lie crossed when at rest, creating an X-shaped pattern on the abdomen. Metamorphosis is partial. The nymphs resemble the adults, but are wingless.

Water bugs may be divided into two groups:
Those living in the water. These have antennae shorter than their head, and their rear pair of legs are often powerful and hairy, for swimming. Most remain in the water as adults.
Those living on the surface of the water. They have long antennae and no swimming legs.

Saucer Bug *Ilyocoris cimicoides*

12-15 mm. Greyish green, broad and flat with a large head sunken into the prothorax. The wings are fully developed, but it does not fly. The forelegs have very thick thighs and are powerful raptorial legs that can fold up like a clasp knife. The middle and rear legs have spines and cilia. It carries a large mass of air both under its elytra and under its body. Its prey includes fish fry, and it can inflict a painful sting! Found locally in shallow water among plants in lakes and slow-moving rivers, particularly in southern regions; active all year.

Aphelocheirus aestivalis

9-12 mm. Resembles a bed bug. Dark on upperside with light border, broad, oval and flat. Head is sunken into prothorax, and wings are hardly developed. Feeds on insect larvae and small bivalves. Breathes using a trapped bubble (plastron) and does not come to the surface. Rather local. It swims around rapidly over gravelly beds of fairly fast-flowing rivers.

egg x 6

nymph

adult

Water Scorpion *Nepa cinerea*

Body 18-22 mm long and approx. 10 mm wide with a long, thin trachea. Greyish brown on upperside, very flat. Abdomen under elytra is pink, as are the wings. Poor swimmer, and drowns if it cannot come up to breathe. Therefore it mainly crawls around on the banks of ponds, lakes and rivers, or sits near the surface on plants in reed swamps with the tip of its breathing tube up in the air. The forelegs are powerful grasping legs that close about its prey like a pocket-knife. It seldom flies, but if there is too little water or not enough to eat, it will fly to another pond. Found in ponds, lakes and slow-moving rivers, and active all year. The eggs, with 7 long thin hairs, are laid just under the surface of the water on moss or algae. The hairs reach to the surface of the water and provide oxygen for the eggs.

Water Stick Insect *Ranatra linearis*

Also known as long-bodied water scorpion. Body 30-35 mm long. Brownish yellow, long and slender. Can swim, but normally lies in wait in ponds with abundant plant life or in reed swamps with the tip of its long breathing tube at the surface. May also sit above the water on floating plants. The forelegs are powerful grasping legs that snap shut on its prey like a pocket-knife. Fairly rare, sensitive to cold and mainly southern.

The eggs are inserted into floating stems of rushes or reed mace in rows, each with two long, white filaments protruding.

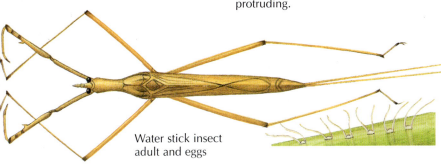

Water stick insect adult and eggs

nymph

> ## Water boatmen
>
> Water boatmen swim on their bellies. They have very short, spoon-shaped forelegs. The rear pair of legs are long, powerful swimming legs that move simultaneously. Air is carried in hairs on the belly, but primarily under the wings, and replaced via a slit between head and prothorax. Their back is flat, and their proboscis inflexible, short and broad, and they cannot sting. They feed mostly on unicellular algae, detritus and rotten plants at the bottom of ponds and slow-moving watercourses with abundant plant life. Their eggs are deposited on the stems of aquatic plants.

egg cocoon x 6

Sigara sp.

7-8 mm. Brown. Striped prothorax (pronotum), and speckled or striped abdomen. Male can produce a loud noise by rubbing the small spines on its front thighs against the side of its head. Rarely flies and is common in ponds, lakes and rivers. Several similar species.

Cymatia sp.

5-6 mm. Very large eyes, and head markedly broader then prothorax. Highly domed forehead. Pronotum is plain brown, without transverse stripes. Two species are common in ponds and slow-moving waters.

Corixa sp.

Up to 16 mm, brownish and flat with black eyes and hairy abdomen. Front pair of legs shaped like scoops and used to churn up the bottom in search of food, especially unicellular algae and rotting plant matter. May also bite holes in algal threads and suck out the chlorophyll granules. The middle pair of legs have powerful claws and are about the same length as the rear pair, which are flat like flippers. Like several other water boatmen, they can make a noise by rubbing their front thighs against the sides of their head. Common in ponds, lakes and slow-moving water with abundant plant life. Active all year and flies well.

Callicorixa sp.

7-8 mm. Brownish black. Head slightly broader than prothorax, which has light transverse stripes. Abdomen closely striped or speckled with small light spots. Male can make an audible noise. Predator that feeds on smaller insect larvae. Active all year. Found locally in ponds, lakes and rivers, and often lives on the bottom. Several similar species.

x 6

Callicorixa sp.

Micronecta sp.

Approx. 2 mm. Pale yellow or grey-white. Flat body with curved sides. Feeds primarily on water fleas. Can make an audible sound, and is fairly common in lakes and slow-moving streams.

x 6

Backswimmers

These elegant bugs swim on their backs, which are keel-shaped like a boat. Air is retained among the fine hairs on the stomach and under the elytra, and they replace it by sticking their abdominal tip up above the surface of the water. They are lighter than water and must work with their rear legs to make their way down through the water. Their eyes are large. They are predators, hunting close to the surface of the water.

Backswimmers bring their legs forward bent, and stretch them out when forcing them quickly backwards, for maximum effect from the 'oar blade' of stiff setae on the legs.

Their large red eyes can see forward, downward and backward at the same time.

When flying to a different site, a backswimmer turns over in the water, breaks the surface film with its back, spreads its wings and takes off with an audible buzzing.

Lesser Backswimmer
Plea sp.

2-2.5 mm. Short, hemispherical body with truncated abdomen. Feeds mainly on water fleas and other small crustaceans. Locally numerous in lakes with rich vegetation and in slow-moving rivers.

x 6

Backswimmer
Notonecta glauca

14-17 mm. Light brown, with dark spot on prothorax and front of abdomen. Often seen at the surface of the water, replacing air. Its forelegs are powerful raptorial legs. Can take large prey, including fish fry, and can inflict a painful bite. Very common all year in ponds, lakes and slow-moving rivers. The nymphs are white or green. Overwinters as adult.

N. lutea, overwinters as an egg.

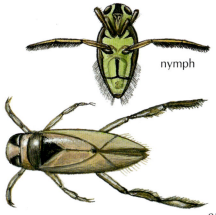

nymph

Pond skaters and relatives

Pond skaters have long antennae and large eyes. They have a very slender body covered with a silvery, water-repellent layer of hair. The thorax is almost as long as the abdomen. They have short forelegs and long, thin middle and rear legs, which they use simultaneously when running briskly and intermittently around, sometimes hopping on the surface of the water. The middle pair of legs propels them forward, the rear ones are used mostly as a rudder. They feed on other insects, particularly terrestrial insects that fall into the water. Overwinters as adult on land. During mating the male perches on top of the female. The nymph has a short, truncated abdomen, only visible as a bulge behind the rear legs.

Water Cricket *Velia caprai*

6-6.5 mm. Brownish, with orange and silvery spots on abdomen, orange on underside. Short, powerful legs that move alternately. Can be winged or wingless. It runs very quickly and is primarily found on streams and rivers with slow-moving currents, particularly in woodland.

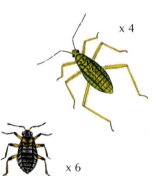

x 4

Mesovelia furcata

3-3.5 mm. Cigar-shaped, glossy green, with long antennae, but no wings. Seen locally, particularly on floating leaves on ponds and lakes.

x 6

x 6

Microvelia pygmaea

1-2 mm. Black with orange spots on thorax and abdomen, has club-shaped antennae and is wingless. Common, primarily on floating leaves and emergent plants on ponds and lakes.

Hebrus pusillus

Approx. 2 mm. Black or reddish head and prothorax. Seen on the banks of ponds in woodland and bogs, running on the leaves of aquatic plants or on the surface of the water.

Water Measurer *Hydrometra stagnorum*

9-12 mm. Very slender, dark brown or black with fila-mentous legs and a long, thin head. Moves slowly and seldom goes out on the open water surface. Common among plants on the banks of ponds, lakes and rivers with a slow-moving current and muddy bottom.

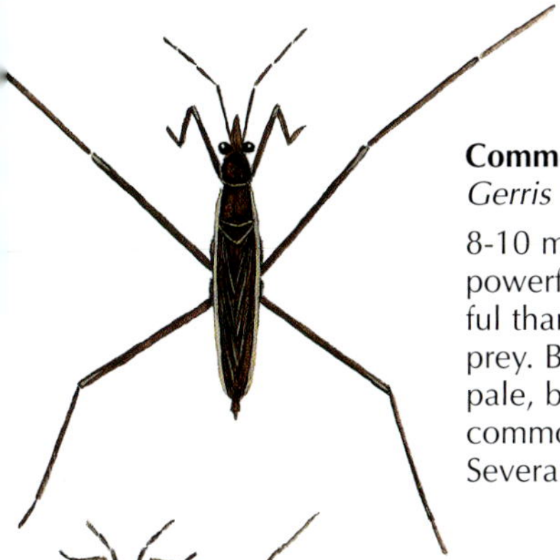

Common Pond Skater
Gerris lacustris

8-10 mm. Brownish-black, slender body and short, powerful proboscis. Forelegs shorter and more power-ful than middle and rear legs, and used for gripping prey. Both winged and wingless forms. The nymph is pale, broad and flat with truncated abdomen. Very common on ponds, lakes and rivers with still water. Several similar species.

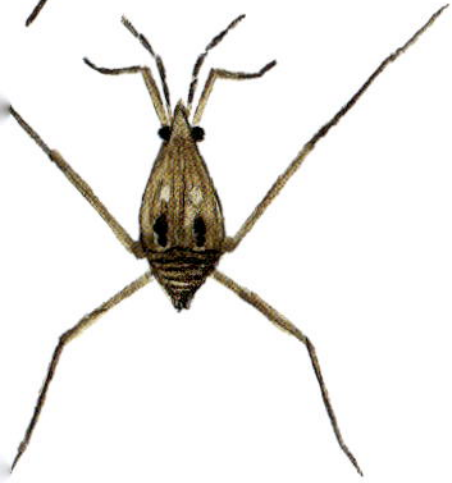

nymph of *Gerris lacustris*

Aquarius najas

13-17 mm. Female larger than male. Greyish black and very powerful, often wingless. Found on slow-moving rivers, particularly in woodland.

97

BEETLES

Beetles have hard, opaque fore-wings (elytra) that cover their entire abdomen like a carapace, except for rove beetles, whose elytra are short. The hind wings are membranous and lie folded under the elytra when not in use. The mouthparts are of the biting sort, and many have elbowed antennae.

Whirligig beetles

Whirligigs are small beetles that swim rapidly in circles on the surface of ponds, lakes and slow-moving rivers, often in large numbers. They have small antennae and short, flattened swimming legs with a large hairy fringe. The eyes are in two parts: the upper half is for viewing above the waterline, the lower half for viewing below the waterline. Air is carried under water as a shining bead around the upperside of the abdominal tip. Flies in autumn, primarily at night, to find new ponds with abundant plant life. The larvae are elongated, with a narrow yellowish head. The abdomen has a pair of filamentous appendages on each segment. Swims like a leech. Pupates, July-August, on land in vegetation in a cocoon of sand grains, plant matter etc. After approx. 10 days the adult beetle emerges. Both larvae and adults are predators, catching primarily small crustaceans and mosquito larvae. The adults also take small animals that have fallen in the water.

Gyrinus sp.

5.6-6.6 mm. Female larger than male. Glossy metallic black with orange legs. Active in the day. Dives down into the water if disturbed. Common on the surface of ponds, lakes and rivers, June-September. Several species.

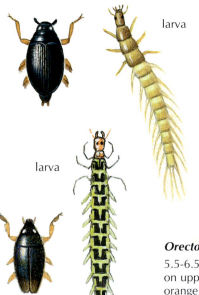

larva

larva

Orectochilus villosus

5.5-6.5 mm. Greyish black or brown with grey hair on upperside. Antennae, legs and underside of body orange. Hides during the day under stones on the edges of lakes or under banks of rivers. Common, particularly on rivers, June-August. Sole European species.

Crawling water beetles

Crawling water beetles are small, extremely convex beetles that live underwater. The head is small and curved with filamentous antennae. The hind coxae extend into broad plates, lying under the abdomen and holding an air cushion. This bubble acts as a physical gill, and the air is rarely renewed. Crawling water beetles can resemble diving beetles, but when swimming they move the two rear pairs of legs alternately as if crawling through the water. They swim slowly among aquatic plants, where both larvae and adults feed on filamentous algae.

Crawling water beetles are closely related to diving beetles.

Haliplus sp.

2.5-2.8 mm. Orange with dark dotted lines and edges on elytra, which are broadest at the shoulders, becoming narrower to the rear. The very large rear coxae lie under the abdomen as plates, holding an air cushion. Lives for several years, overwinters in water. Common in reed swamps in shallow water in ponds, lakes and slow-moving rivers, May-July.
Larva, up to 12 mm, with somewhat curved head and long tail. Moves slowly, creeping among aquatic plants. Pupates on land and remains there until early summer.

Brychius elevatus

3.5-4.5 mm. Yellow with dark dotted lines and ribs on elytra. Curved head. Found in ponds, ditches, and reed swamps in shallow water in lakes. May-July.

Noterus crassicornis

A diving beetle. 3-4 mm. Yellowish brown to brick-red. Convex, egg-shaped body, broadest at front. Feeds on smaller insects and small crustaceans. Very common at the bottom of reed swamps in shallow water in ponds and lakes and in large streams. Larva, up to 8 mm, pale yellow with brownish head and biting mouthparts. Short, powerful legs with no swimming setae. Found half-buried in mud in fairly shallow water with its abdominal tip above the surface of the water. Feeds on small insect larvae.

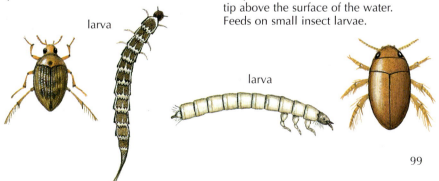

larva

larva

Diving beetles

Diving beetles are generally slightly convex beetles with sharp edges. They have a head partially sunken into their thorax, filamentous antennae and large eyes. The adults carry air in a cavity under their elytra. They renew the air by sticking their abdominal tip up through the surface of the water. They have well-developed hind wings and fly, primarily at night. Their legs each have two claws. Their rear legs are flat, and hairy for swimming, and move simultaneously. In many species the males have swollen forefeet. Most are found all year round. Both adults and larvae are predators.

The larva has a forward-pointing head with powerful mandibles. It injects poison from its mandibles into its prey, disabling it and partially dissolving its inner organs. Its abdomen has two tail filaments.

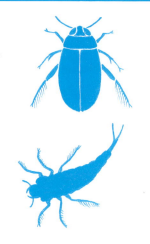

Ilybius ater

13-14 mm. Large, black and convex, broadest towards the rear and blackish brown on underside. Reddish antennae and legs. Common in ponds and lakes.

Ilybius finestratus

8.5-14 mm. Large and convex. Black with reddish sheen on upperside. Red on underside. Found April-October in ponds and lakes, occasionally streams, with abundant plant life.

Ilybius fuliginosus

10 mm. Dark bronze-coloured. Reddish-brown sides to prothorax. Elytra have yellowish side stripe that forks at the back. Common in lakes and rivers.

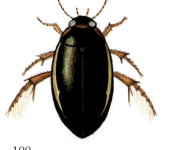

Platambus maculatus

7-8 mm. Head and prothorax reddish with dark edges. Elytra yellowish with bold dark markings, broad longitudinal stripes and spots. Underside, legs and antennae rust-red. Very common, particularly on sandy, stony bottoms of lakes and major rivers, and in brackish water, June-October.
The larva, up to 10 mm, has a light-brown head with 'bandit mask', a dark-brown transverse band with two light spots. The thorax also has a dark transverse band with light spots. Found primarily in hollows on stones etc. and among pondweed in slightly deeper water.

larva

larva

Agabus paludosus

7 mm. Two light spots on head. Sides of prothorax yellowish brown. Elytra dark brown with lighter sides. Common in woodland streams and rivers.
The larva, up to 12.5 mm, is brown to olive-brown with light spots. No cilia on legs. Common June-August.

Agabus guttatus

8 mm. Dark brown or black. Elytra have two blurred yellow patches towards the rear and two small round yellow spots at the tip. Found locally in springs and stony woodland streams, particularly on the undersides of stones in June.

Most diving beetles can live for several years, and lay eggs every year.

Agabus undulatus

Approx. 7.5 mm. Black prothorax. Elytra dark brown with yellow spots. Underside reddish, antennae and legs rust-red. Fairly common among plants in ponds and lakes, especially in and near woodland.

Laccophilus minutus

4-4.5 mm. Fairly flat. Brownish-yellow head and thorax. Elytra have greenish sheen and indistinct darker spots, or completely green with light spots. Rear legs have distinct lobes. Common in ponds and lakes. About three species of this genus occur in Britain.

Hyphydrus ovatus

4.5-5 mm. Rust-red, short and broad with extremely convex upper and underside. Very common nearly all year in ponds and lakes with abundant plant life, particularly in woodland.

The larva, up to 7.7 mm, has yellowish-brown head with two dark longitudinal stripes. First thorax segment and the two front and two rear abdominal segments are whitish. The rest of the body is dark brown or black. The larva runs round on the bottom or on plants after prey, particularly small crustaceans. Common June-August.

x 3

larva

The eyes of a diving beetle larva are visible as 6 dark spots on the side of the head. They cannot form images, they can only see movement and distinguish between light and dark.

larva

larva

Hygrotus **sp.**

3.5 mm. Short, egg-shaped, very convex with fairly large eyes. Yellow elytra with black edges and black, often short, merged and broken longitudinal lines. Very common in ponds and lakes, particularly in woodland, but may also be found in slow-moving water.

The larva, up to 5 mm, is light greyish brown with dark rear edge to segments. Dark spot on head, spindle-shaped, light longitudinal stripe on prothorax. Common June-August.

Hydroporus sp.

3-5 mm. Reddish brown, yellow or orange with dark patches of variable size. Approx. 25 species, which are very common in ponds, lakes and slow-moving water. A large genus with some 50 species in Britain.

Oreodytes sanmarkii

3 mm. Short and broad. Yellow on upperside with black or brown, often partially merged longitudinal lines on elytra. Black underside. Legs and antennae yellow. Found in stony streams; often sits on stones.

Scarodytes halensis

4-4.5 mm. Head and thorax orange with black markings. Ochre-yellow elytra with black seam and black, short, partially merging, longitudinal lines. Found rivers and ponds, particularly on clay.

Nebrioporus depressus

4.5 mm. Orange. Black rear edge on head. Black markings at rear of prothorax. Black, often broken, short or partially merging longitudinal lines on elytra, which have a peg at the tip. Common in rivers and large lakes with sandy banks.
The larva, up to 6.5 mm, is spindle-shaped and pale with a brown-spotted back. Cilia on all tibiae and on middle and rear thighs and ankle joints.

larva from above

Rhantus exoletus

9-10 mm. Head and prothorax orange with black markings. Elytra yellowish brown with dense, green marbling, yellow underside. Found in ponds and lakes.

Colymbetes fuscus

16-17 mm. Slender, oval body. Head black or brown, prothorax black with brownish-yellow sides. Elytra yellowish brown with dense, fine green transverse stripes and yellow edges. Common in ditches, ponds and lakes with abundant plant life.

When swimming, a diving beetle holds its first pair of legs close in to its body. These are the short grasping legs, used to hold its prey firmly while eating it. The second pair of legs is used when sitting and holding tight to aquatic plants etc. The rear pair are broad and flat like a pair of oars, and used for propulsion.

Hydaticus transversalis

12-13 mm. Black with broad reddish border, which has dark stripes at rear of elytra. Two reddish transverse patches at front of elytra. Found locally in ponds, ditches, marshes etc. spring and autumn.

Graphoderes sp.

13-15 mm. Yellow head with black streaks, yellow prothorax with broad black transverse band at front and back. Brownish-yellow elytra with green or black marbling. Upper and underside almost smooth. Male has 2-3 very large suckers and numerous small ones on its forefeet.

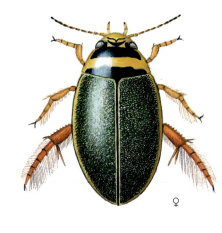

♀

♀

Acilius sulcatus

16-18 mm. Yellowish brown, broad, slightly convex. Yellow prothorax with two black transverse bands that are merged in females. Elytra densely speckled with black spots. Female's elytra have four light hairy furrows and five dark longitudinal ribs. Fairly common in marshes, ponds, lakes and slow-moving water, especially May-July. Eggs are laid in clumps on land. The larva, up to 30 mm, is yellowish brown or greenish, speckled with brown and black spots. Elongated prothorax (pronotum), giving long-necked impression. Fairly thick abdomen. Has cilia on its legs and swims after its prey.

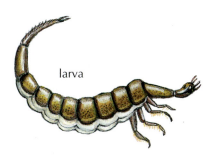

larva

♂   ♀

Great Diving Beetle
Dytiscus marginalis

30-35 mm. Reddish brown with dark-green sheen. Prothorax and elytra have yellow border. Male has broad forefeet and finely-dotted, smooth, glossy elytra. Female is slightly smaller with elytra that are either less glossy, more markedly and densely dotted or longi-tudinally-furrowed with lighter colouring in the furrows. Common in ponds and lakes with abundant plant life, often in or near woodland.

The larva, up to 50 mm, has a large head and powerful mandibles and is capable of catching even large prey such as tadpoles, newt larvae and small fish. Brown body with broad yellow or yellowish-brown central line and indistinct yellowish-brown spots at sides. Good swimmer. Thick hair fringes along sides of legs and abdomen. Seen primarily in spring and early summer in deep water suspended in an S-shape from the surface film with legs extended to sides and its piercing, dag-ger-like mandibles pointing forward.

Diving beetle larvae pupate in a small hole in soft soil near the water's edge. After a few weeks the adult beetle emerges. Overwinters as adult in water and lays eggs in spring, usually in water.

larva

Scavenger beetles

Scavenger beetles have short antennae ending in a fine hairy club. They have prominent palps that are often longer than their antennae. Body shape varies greatly, but the underside is densely covered with hair, which retains air and is therefore always silvery underwater. They move their legs alternately. The adults only feed on fresh green aquatic plants. Females have silk glands and lay eggs in watertight cocoons.
The larvae can vary greatly in appearance. They sometimes have warts on their abdomen, but all have three pairs of legs. They are fairly slow, and often sit on aquatic plants head downwards and abdominal tip just above the water. Some eat algae, but most are predators. Pupation takes place in soil on land.

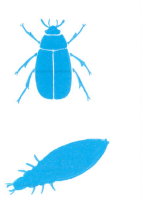

Hydrophilus aterrimus

32-40 mm. Glossy black with a green sheen; both upper and underside are convex. Elytra have distinct rows of dots. Long spines on tibia. Flat middle and rear feet with cilia on inside. Fairly common in ponds with muddy bottoms.
Lays 60-70 eggs in cocoons, up to 24 mm in diameter, with a beak-shaped 'neck', that float on the surface of the water covered by a leaf, duckweed etc. Air gets to the eggs through the 'neck'.
The larva, up to 60 mm, is grey to grey-brown. Feeds primarily on snails. Development takes several years. It overwinters in water, but pupates in a hole on land.

The larva of *Hydrophilus* uses external digestion: it spits gastric juice over its prey to break it down before it can suck up the decomposed matter. They feed mainly on water snails, but some species take worms and other larvae as well. The largest British water beetle is *Hydrophilus piceus*, the Great Silver Diving Beetle, which reaches almost 50 mm. Although vegetarian, it can inflict a prick with the sharp spine on its underside and should be handled with care. Found locally in still waters, mainly in the south.

larva

Spercheus emarginatus

5.5-7 mm. Brownish-yellow elytra with dark spots, broadest, almost angular, in centre. Short prothorax that narrows in front of elytra. Female carries eggs in a cocoon below her belly. Found locally in small ponds with abundant plant life. Roams around on the underside of the water surface.

The larva is short and broad with a flat underside and convex upperside. Brown head and thorax, greyish abdomen. It is very hairy, and the abdomen has a pair of hairy warts on each segment. Large, crescent-shaped mandibles, and, like the adult, the larva hangs under the surface film and sweeps with its jaws for small particles, crustaceans etc.

larva

Helochares griseus

4.5-6.5 mm. Oblong and only slightly convex, brownish yellow on upperside with dark spots and longitudinal lines. Underside black. Antennae and legs brownish yellow. Female carries her egg cocoon under her belly, and so the air mass is under the breast and head. Very common in ponds and lakes. The sole British species is *H. lividus.*

Scavenger beetles are poor swimmers. They move their legs alternately and most crawl across the bottom among aquatic plants, or 'walk' through the water. Small species often swim belly upward due to the air held under the body, or run around on the underside of the water surface.

Helophorus aquaticus

6-9 mm. Five pronounced longitudinal grooves on prothorax. Head narrows behind eyes. Elytra brown with rows of dots, prothorax has a bronze sheen. Antennae short, tibia fairly slim with longitudinal rows of fine spines and a distinct terminal spur. Common in ditches, ponds and lakes and often seen above water on the bank. Swarms above water on warm summer evenings. Large genus.

Enochrus sp.

5.5-6.5 mm. Oblong and convex. Forehead between eyes is very dark. Brownish-yellow upperside and black underside. Small black spots on prothorax, surrounding an indistinct dark patch. The elytra sometimes have a dark shoulder patch. Common in ponds and lakes. Several similar species in this large genus.

Hydrobius fuscipes

6-7.5 mm. Glossy black, or totally or partially brownish. Antennae, palps, tibia and feet reddish brown. Distinct dotted stripes on elytra. Locally common in ponds, lakes and rivers, where it crawls around among plants in shallow water. Lays 13-20 eggs in white urn-shaped cocoons, approx. 4 mm long, with ruff-shaped link to floating leaves, moss etc.

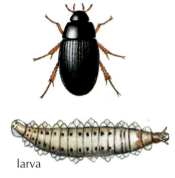

The larva, up to 15 mm, is brownish white on upperside of abdomen with dark spots at front and rear, and greyish on underside. Head and thorax dark brown. Often found near the surface of the water and feeds on small crustaceans, such as ostracods and copepods. Pupates in a small hole in damp soil near water.

larva

Scavenger beetles replace air by bringing their head up to the surface. Their antennae clubs and the hairs on the sides of their head then form an air duct down to the bubble held under the abdomen.

Hydrochara caraboides

14-18 mm. Elongated, convex and egg-shaped in outline. Glossy black with a greenish sheen and dense hair on underside. Good swimmer and resembles a small *Hydrophilus*. Female lays eggs in cocoons like those of *Hydrophilus* (p.107), but smaller.

Ochthebius sp.

1.8-2 mm. Upperside dark bronze-coloured and sometimes brownish at rear. Protruding eyes. Palps shorter than its reddish antennae. Pronounced dotted stripes on elytra, body narrows between prothorax and elytra. Entire underside is covered by a large air mass. Found in ponds and lakes and also seen on damp ground near the bank. Found also in saline puddles. Often moves about on the underside of the surface film.

Hydraena sp.

2.2-2.4 mm. Elongated, with glossy, black or brownish upperside which narrows between prothorax and elytra. Antennae, palps and legs reddish; palps much longer then antennae. Common, particularly in stony wood-land streams, where it perches on branches or stones.

Limnebius sp.

1.7-2 mm. Oval and black, with no narrowing be-tween prothorax and elytra. Two small bristles on tip of tail. Found in both running and standing water.

Hydrochus sp.

2.5-4.3 mm. Head and prothorax black or green. Pro-truding eyes; large hollows on prothorax. Elytra, usually very dark, occasionally green, have pro-nounced dotted lines between high longitudinal ridges. Fairly common, primarily in spring in ponds with abundant plant life.

Anacaena sp.

2.3-2.8 mm. Short, broad and highly convex, often brown and glossy. Legs hairy, except outer third. Very common in all kinds of fresh water; can also live in brackish water.

Cymbiodyta marginella

3-4 mm. Elongated and somewhat convex, black with brownish-yellow border. Palps very long. Found in ponds and lakes.

Laccobius sp.

3-3.5 mm. Oval and convex with two yellow spots in front of eyes. Large black spot on prothorax, and two light spots on elytra. Common in ponds, lakes and rivers. Several species.

Berosus luridus

3.5-4.8 mm. Highly convex eyes. Narrows between prothorax and elytra. Upperside brownish yellow, and elytra often have indistinct dark patches. Palps, antennae and legs orange. Mid and hind legs have swimming hairs. Fairly common in stagnant pools and ponds, and also found in brackish water, particularly in small ponds in saltmarshes. Very active.
The larva has yellow cilia on all its legs and long, thin tracheal gills. Does not come to the surface to breathe. Several species in Britain.

larva

Elodes minuta

4.5-6 mm. Orange, broad and very flat. Filamentous antennae, black or brown at tip. Elytra brownish yellow with a dark tip that often extends forward somewhat on back, but elytra may also be completely black. Found among plants near streams and on stones in springs in early summer. Sometimes moves under the surface of the water.
The larva, up to 6.5 mm, is brown, broad and flat, with long antennae covered with fine setae. The head extends into 'ears' that also bear setae.

larva

111

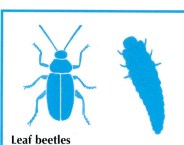

Leaf beetles

Leaf beetles are often boldly coloured and shiny, with an extremely convex body like ladybirds, but longer antennae. They feed on leaves and are often specific to a particular plant. The larvae are soft and have one or two spiny protuberances towards the tip of the abdomen. They are found in stems or roots, and can make tunnels or live in the open on leaves and roots of aquatic and marsh plants. Large family, a few of which have aquatic larvae.

Donacia sp.

5.5-13 mm. Elongated body, usually with metallic sheen of clear, golden, red, green or blue. Protruding eyes and long antennae shaped like strings of pearls. Flattened elytra, often blunt at end. Underside densely hairy. Male more slender than female, with longer antennae and more powerful legs. Found on various aquatic plants, but mainly seen in reed swamps in sunny weather.

The larvae, up to 15 mm, are found on roots, where they suck air from the plant through two spines on the 8th abdominal section. The pupa is thick-skinned, brown and found on roots.

Donacia sp. on reed

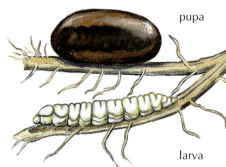

pupa

larva

Galerucella nymphaea

6-7 mm. Oblong body, both upperside and underside very hairy. Head is orange at front, black at rear, with protruding eyes and long antennae resembling strings of beads. Orange prothorax with black or dark lateral hollows and a black, smooth central part. Black or blackish-brown elytra with orange edges, but may be yellowish-brown or reddish-brown. Orange legs. Common on water-lily leaves.

The larva, up to 10 mm, is black with yellowish-green transverse stripes and pale belly. Lives on upperside of water-lily leaves, amphibious bistort and marsh cinquefoil, where it gnaws thin, approx. 1 mm-wide, winding tunnels on upperside of leaf.

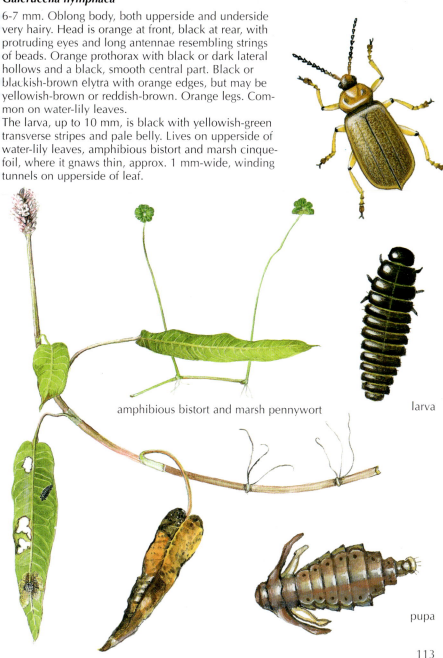

amphibious bistort and marsh pennywort

larva

pupa

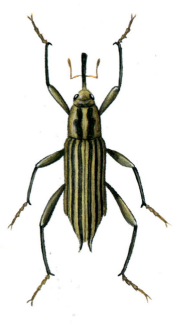

Weevils

The front part of a weevil's head is elongated like a snout, with the mouthparts at the tip. The body is often thick and round, and the antennae are usually elbowed and club-tipped. The larvae are pale and legless, resembling maggots. They live either in the ground, feeding on plant roots, or in leaves, stems, roots or fruits. A few of them are specific to aquatic plants.

Dicranthus elegans

5.5-7.5 mm. Elongate, with two long, pointed spines on elytra. Upperside is greyish yellow and scaly with two broad longitudinal bands on prothorax and several black or blackish-brown stripes on elytra. Long legs. Antennae and feet reddish. Snout only slightly curved. Found locally underwater on reeds in ponds and lakes. The larva lives in the reeds.

Thryogenes nereis

4-5 mm. Oblong-shaped body and fairly long snout. Common in ponds, lakes and rivers on club-rushes and spike-rushes.
The larva lives in the stems, where it also pupates.

Limnobaris pilistriata

2.8-4.5 mm. Black, slender body, fine greyish hair on upperside, and white or yellow scales along sides on underside. Elytra only slightly wider than prothorax. Powerful legs with large claws. Found on sedges, club-rushes and rushes, where the larva lives in the crown.

Bagous glabriostris

An aquatic weevil. 2.3-3.2mm. Broad with long legs. Upperside brownish or greyish. Elytra striped and clearly broader than prothorax. Tibia, feet and base of antennae reddish. The adult beetle, the larva and pupa found locally on the aquatic plant water soldier and possibly also on pondweed and water plantain in ponds, lakes and rivers.

Bagous tempestivus

An aquatic weevil. 2.8-3 mm. Elongated body and slender legs. Elytra have parallel sides at front and are broader than prothorax. Two dark longitudinal bands on prothorax. Dark stripes and light transverse bands on elytra. Found locally in ponds, lakes and rivers on sedge, pondweed and arrowhead, where larvae and pupae can also be seen.

Litodactylus leucogaster

2.4-3.2 mm. Black with reddish legs and antennae. Underside is densely covered with white scales. Upperside is covered by brown and white scales with fairly clear spots. The adult lives underwater on water milfoil in summer, but overwinters on land. Found locally in ponds and lakes.
The larva lives on the leaves and makes an underwater cocoon on the plant.

Tanysphyrus lemnae

1.5-1.8 mm. Black with lighter antennae and legs. Two light spots at rear of prothorax and two longitudinal bands. Longitudinally-grooved elytra, also with white spots, but more indistinct. Found on the leaves of dense masses of duckweed in village ponds and other nutrient-rich waters, primarily spring and autumn. Overwinters as adult.
The larva mines duckweed leaves, moving from leaf to leaf. It can be found in midsummer.

larva on duckweed

Rove beetles

Rove beetles are elongate and mostly fairly small and lively, and their larvae resemble those of ground beetles. They have rather short elytra, which often only cover the first two abdominal segments, but most have well-developed wings and can fly well. The abdomen is very flexible. Most are predators, but many feed on animal dung, carrion, fungi and rotten plants.

Stenus bimaculatus

Approx. 5 mm. Steel-blue with large protruding eyes, two red spots on elytra and orange legs. Dense hair on body. Active in the day and found among plants on the banks of lakes and large ponds. From a gland in its abdomen it can secrete a fluid that alters the surface tension, so that it shoots across the water like a rocket. Hunts springtails etc. by darting its sticky tongue out to approx. 1/3 of its length.

Stenus sp. Several species of this genus are common in fresh water.

x 3

Paederus litoralis

7.5-8.5 mm. Head black, thorax and most of abdomen orange. Elytra metallic green. Abdominal tip bluish black. Cannot fly. Predator. Usually lives among withered leaves etc. in marshes and on the banks of lakes and rivers, and near beaches. Uncommon.

Elaphrus riparius

A ground beetle. 6.5-8 mm. Green with lighter circular spots on elytra, and green feet. However, elytra can be metallic blue or shiny bronze. Runs quickly and often flies. Found mainly in sunny weather on damp clayey or sandy soil with sparse vegetation near standing or slow-moving water, particularly in June.

x 3

Riffle beetles

Riffle beetles cannot swim, but their legs have long, powerful claws, so they can hold on to stones and plants underwater. They are also seen on plants above the water. They are small and black. The head is curved, with long, filamentous antennae. Riffle beetles breathe via a physical gill (plastron) and feed on algae, fungi, bacteria, detritus etc. The larvae are brownish with short antennae and legs. They are slow and take the same food as the adults. Pupation takes place on land.

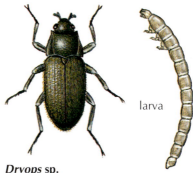

larva

Dryops sp.

4.5-5.5 mm. Elongate, highly convex and very hairy. Antennae very short and thick. Dark prothorax. Elytra are finely hairy and can be plain greyish brown or have dark spots. Common in lakes in plants near the bank.
The larva, up to 9 mm, is light brown, elongate, with a few scattered setae and short, powerful legs. Found in submerged wood, where it feeds.

Elmis aenea

1.5-2.5 mm. Black, often with a bronze sheen. Antennae brown with lighter base. Feet also light. Two longitudinal grooves on prothorax that meet ahead of elytra. Numerous keeled longitudinal grooves on elytra. Common among plants in moderately fast-flowing streams and rivers.
The larva, up to 3.5 mm, is broad, flattened, and pointed at rear end. Upperside is grainy and has powerful hairy protuberances along the sides. Found on stones in fast-flowing water. Pupates in a little hole in the ground on land.

Limnius volckmari

2.8-3.2 mm. Black with a bronze-like sheen. Antennae light at base. Two longitudinal grooves on prothorax that do not meet ahead of elytra. No keeled longitudinal grooves on elytra. Common in moderate to fast-flowing streams and rivers.
The larva, up to 6 mm, is elongate and cylindrical, brownish yellow and grainy.

larva

larva

larva

larva

Oulimnius sp.

1.5-1.7 mm. Dark bronze with brownish underside and orange antennae and legs. Two longitudinal grooves on prothorax, not connected at rear. Felt-like hair along sides of prothorax and elytra. Common in lakes and rivers. Two very similar species in the region.

The larva, up to 2.5 mm, is greyish brown, fairly flat, with a pointed abdominal tip. Upperside is densely covered with small nodules.

Riolus cupreus

1.5-2.0 mm. Dark brown, often with a bronze metallic sheen. Underside, antennae and legs brownish. No longitudinal grooves on prothorax, but elytra have pronounced dotted lines with raised sections. Found locally in the splash zone in lakes and strong-flowing water.

The larva, up to 3 mm, is almost cylindrical.

SPRINGTAILS

Springtails are small insects with a distinct head, two antennae and three pairs of legs. Most springtails have a spring-like appendage (furcula) on their abdomen that is triggered when the insect is disturbed, shooting it up into the air. Most feed on organic material, but a few are predators. A few live on the water surface.

The male discharges its sperm in capsules, spermatophores. These float like boats on the surface of the water, and the male pursues the females, almost thrusting the spermatophores at them.

x 15

Podura aquatica

1.2 mm. Steel-blue, dumpy and wingless, with short antennae, three pairs of short legs and a spring-like furcula flat under the body. Young may be pink or reddish. When the insect is disturbed, the furcula is forced powerfully down and back and shoots the insect forward in a long somersault. Feeds on rotting plant matter, bacteria, pollen etc., and is an important food for pond skaters and the like. Common, and often in large numbers on the surface or close to the banks of ponds and lakes with still water.

Water mites

These mites, that have adapted to life in fresh water, are often boldly coloured red or green. Mostly found in ponds and lakes, but also in unpolluted springs. Water mites have a six-legged larval stage, parasitising aquatic insects (especially dragonflies, mosquitoes and beetles) and bivalves etc. The nymphs and adults have eight legs and live as predators, feeding on aquatic insects and their eggs, small crustaceans etc. During the free-living stages they swim actively in the water aided by the long cilia on their legs. There are some 900 species in Europe, of which around 300 occur in Britain.

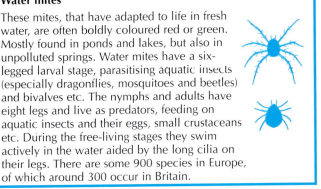

larvae on pond skater x 1

Diplodontus despiciens

Approx. 2 mm. Reddish brown and spherical with dark spots on its back. Wide variation. Common in ponds and lakes among plants. The larvae parasitise mosquitoes.

x 4

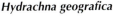

Limnochares aquaticus

4 mm. Blood-red, large and fat. Short legs with no cilia. Body almost rectangular, soft-skinned and rubbery. Common in lakes, and crawls slowly around on the bottom in shallow water among plants. The larvae parasitise dragonflies and pond skaters and are seen as 'red buds' on their legs.

Above, a water mite. Members of this group can be difficult to identify.

Hydrachna geografica

6-7 mm. A large species. Spherical, with fairly powerful swimming legs, red with large angular spots. Found locally among plants in ponds and lakes in shallow water. The larvae parasitise diving beetles.

x 4

♂

Arrenurus sp.

1-2 mm. Female is circular; male often has a narrow, elongated abdomen. Swimming legs fairly long and green, with stiff swimming setae. Some species are green with brown back markings, others are reddish with a green marking on the body. Common in small ponds with abundant plant life and among plants in lakes and streams. The larvae parasitise mosquitoes, dragonflies and caddis flies.

Unionicola ypsilophora

Unionicola crassipes

1-1.5 mm. Yellowish, with two small spots and three dark-brown markings on back. Very long legs with long swimming setae. Found locally free-swimming in lakes. Feeds on small crustaceans. The larvae parasitise bivalves, freshwater snails and sponges. ***U. ypsilophora*** is a closely related species.

Water mite larvae can be found on various aquatic insects: on pond skaters they are seen as 'red buds' on the body or legs, on mosquitoes and aquatic beetles they settle particularly on the thorax or between the head and thorax. As the larvae are parasites on adult aquatic insects, they must quickly find their way back to their host, when they shed their skin, or when they metamorphose from pupa into adult insect. By attaching themselves to the adult insects they achieve effective dispersal.

Hydrozetes lacustris, a beetle mite. Common in lakes etc. x 50

water mite egg mass

Spiders

Spiders have eight legs, a small sturdy thorax, and a large, soft abdomen. All spiders have spinnerets. They are predators, some capturing their prey in a web, while others lie in wait, or run or jump after their prey, which is then paralysed with poison injected through fangs. Eggs are laid in a silken cell, guarded by the female. The young develop to sexual maturity through several moults.

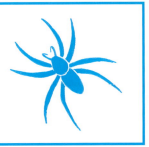

Raft Spider *Dolomedes fimbriatus*

Female 13-20 mm, male 9-15 mm. Also known (more aptly) as 'Fishing Spider' or 'Swamp Spider'. Dark-brown thorax and legs. Abdomen black with small, light spots and a brown central stripe halfway down the upperside. Thorax and abdomen have two pale yellow lines along the sides. Runs very fast on the water surface, catching animals that have fallen in the water, but it can also go underwater to catch fish larvae, tadpoles etc. Air is trapped in a thin layer of hairs around the body; the spider often creeps into the water if disturbed. The mating period is in July. The eggs are carried in a round cocoon beneath the thorax, and the tiny spiderlings are brought to land in a large nursery tent, guarded by the female. Occurs locally on shores of ponds, lakes, bogs and pools. It has an extremely painful bite, but is very shy. There are two species, both widepread in northern Europe. In Britain, *D. fimbriatus* is local and rather southern, but the similar *D. plantarius* is very rare and known only from a few fenland sites in East Anglia and Sussex.

'diving bell'

Water Spider
Argyroneta aquatica

Female 8-15 mm, male 9-12 mm. Red-brown thorax and legs, body almost smooth. Grey-black abdomen. The only truly aquatic spider. Moves among plants or swims on its back at an angle by paddling with its legs. The underside of the thorax and the entire abdomen look silvery, due to a layer of air trapped by hairs. By day it stays in a shining, dome-shaped 'diving bell' filled with air among aquatic plants near the surface. By night it hunts on the bottom. Feeds primarily on water slaters and insect larvae. Has a painful bite. Female extends the bell at the top into a brood chamber. Lives several years and overwinters in a closed bell or an empty snail shell, which it fills with air and seals shut. These snail shells can occasionally be spotted drifting on the surface or frozen in ice in winter. Occurs locally in ponds and bogs with abundant plant life.

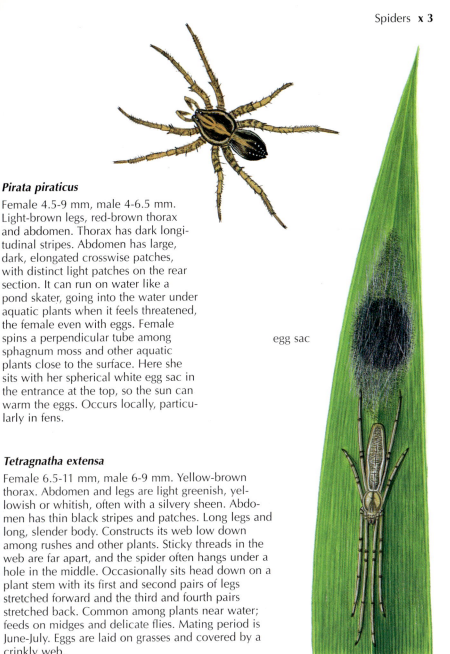

egg sac

Pirata piraticus

Female 4.5-9 mm, male 4-6.5 mm.
Light-brown legs, red-brown thorax
and abdomen. Thorax has dark longitudinal stripes. Abdomen has large,
dark, elongated crosswise patches,
with distinct light patches on the rear
section. It can run on water like a
pond skater, going into the water under
aquatic plants when it feels threatened,
the female even with eggs. Female
spins a perpendicular tube among
sphagnum moss and other aquatic
plants close to the surface. Here she
sits with her spherical white egg sac in
the entrance at the top, so the sun can
warm the eggs. Occurs locally, particularly in fens.

Tetragnatha extensa

Female 6.5-11 mm, male 6-9 mm. Yellow-brown
thorax. Abdomen and legs are light greenish, yellowish or whitish, often with a silvery sheen. Abdomen has thin black stripes and patches. Long legs and
long, slender body. Constructs its web low down
among rushes and other plants. Sticky threads in the
web are far apart, and the spider often hangs under a
hole in the middle. Occasionally sits head down on a
plant stem with its first and second pairs of legs
stretched forward and the third and fourth pairs
stretched back. Common among plants near water;
feeds on midges and delicate flies. Mating period is
June-July. Eggs are laid on grasses and covered by a
crinkly web.

CRUSTACEANS

Noble Crayfish
Astacus astacus

Female up to approx. 12 cm long, male up to approx. 16 cm. Female has broader tail, male has larger claws.
5 pairs of walking limbs: the first has large claws, the second and third pair small. The tail is large, with a fan formed by a pair of enlarged abdominal limbs. It hides away during the day under stones or in holes dug in the bank.

Mating takes place September-November. Eggs, 50-350, are laid 3-6 weeks later and stick fast to the female's pleopods. 20-25 eggs hatch May-June. They are approx. 10 mm long and have a thick body with no tail fan.

> Crayfish do not like acidic or polluted water, and most species are restricted to clean, flowing water.

> Crayfish are preyed on mainly by eels, pike, perch, burbot, trout, herons, mink and otters.

They cling to the female's pleopods for the first 10-15 days.
Noble crayfish moult eight times in their first year, five times in their second year and three times in their third year. Males become sexually mature in their third year, females in their fourth. Females subsequently moult once a year, males twice. The skin takes a week to harden. They eat the discarded skin to provide calcium for their new one. Noble Crayfish can live to approx. 15 years old.

This species is widespread in northern, central and eastern Europe, but absent from Britain and Ireland. It prefers shallow water on a firm substrate in ponds, lakes and waterways, where the water is pure and well oxygenated. The natural range has been extended by introductions.

The native British species, also found in lowland France and Belgium, is the White-clawed Crayfish *(Austropotamobius pallipes)*; it is somewhat smaller.

The native European crayfish species have been wiped out in many places by crayfish disease, which is caused by a fungus. Signal Crayfish are only affected to a slight extent by this disease and can therefore spread it to White-clawed and Noble Crayfish.

Branchiobdella astaci

Up to 12 mm. This is not a leech, but a leech-like, brownish worm. It lacks bristles, and has biting mouthparts and a sucker at the rear end. An external parasite on crayfish. Feeds on the crayfish's blood and is found primarily on the gills. Seen locally in crayfish populations, though rare in Britain.

x 4

Small crayfish often lie hidden under stones on the banks of ponds and lakes. They are not difficult to catch by hand.

Larger crayfish are caught at night using crayfish cages, pots or dipping nets with a cut-up dead fish or a piece of flesh as bait.

Although they are farmed in many places in Europe, crayfish are becoming rarer in Britain and should not be collected.

Signal Crayfish
Pacifastacus leniusculus

Grows rapidly, becoming slightly larger and more powerful than noble crayfish. Male has larger claws and female broader tail than the noble crayfish. The claw has a conspicuous white spot. In older animals this spot may be bluish on the upperside of the claw. Adults eat mainly plants. Females lay 200-400 eggs, of which approx. 100 hatch. The young are sexually mature after approximately two years. Found in many places, including ponds and lakes. Are better able to tolerate nutrient-rich water and greater temperature fluctuations than Noble Crayfish. Signal Crayfish originate from North America, but have been introduced in many places. Due to its rapid growth, greater fertility and less demanding habitat requirements it can outcompete the native species, partly because the latter are more at risk from the disease which the Signal Crayfish brought with it.

Crayfish have red, blue, green and yellow pigments in their skin, giving a brownish shade. When cooked they turn red, as all the other pigments are destroyed by the heat.

Freshwater shrimps

Shrimps are fairly large crustaceans with a compressed body. The first thorax segment is fused with the head. The free thorax segments and the abdominal segments all have limbs. The rear three on the thorax are used for walking. The tail and the first three flat, bristle-bearing pleopods are used for swimming, and the last three are for jumping. The male is larger than the female, which carries the eggs in a brood pouch under the body.

Spiny-headed worms

Spiny-headed worms live as parasites in the intestinal tract of vertebrates, particularly fish and birds. They are elongated and round with a long abdomen and short thorax, consisting of a neck and proboscis, with a multitude of hooks. They are unisexual, and males are normally much smaller than females, which produce thousands of eggs a day. The larvae develop in the eggs, but are discharged with the host's droppings and continue to develop in the body cavity of an intermediate host, either a crustacean or an insect.

Echinorrhyncus sp.

A spiny-headed worm. Larva approx. 2 mm. Red. Often seen under the carapace of freshwater shrimps. Adults live in the intestines of aquatic birds, particularly ducks and moorhens. There can be as many as 1,000 in a single intestine.

Common Freshwater Shrimp *Gammarus pulex*
Male up to 20 mm, female much smaller. Very common in shallow water among plants and under stones etc. in all types of fresh water. In strong currents it seeks shelter behind stones and among plants. Probably the most important food for numerous fish and other predators.

Gammarus lacustris

Male approx. 20 mm, female much smaller. Dark green with a red spot on the side of the first three abdominal segments, if infected with the parasite *Echinorrhyncus.* Common in large lakes and some watercourses. Difficult to distinguish from the common freshwater shrimp.

Pallasea quadrispinosa

Male up to 17 mm, female much
smaller. Yellowish green to brownish
grey with a distinct brownish-green
stripe on each segment. Powerful
spines on 1st or 2nd abdominal segment. Found locally in large lakes in
northern Europe, but not in Britain.
Swims around among plants at a depth
of 4-7 metres in summer. Found in
shallower water in winter.

Pontoporeia affinis

Up to 8 mm. White. Breeds in winter and early
spring. Found on the bottom in the deep lakes and
estuaries flowing into the Baltic and Arctic seas. Not
found in Britain. Possibly a relict from the Ice Age.

Opossum Shrimp *Mysis relicta*

Up to 14 mm, elongate, with large
stalked eyes, a carapace over the thorax
and a swimming fan on tip of tail. It has
8 pairs of thoracic legs that are forked
swimming legs. Female carries the eggs
in a brood pouch between the legs. An
Ice Age relict, inhabits deep cool lakes in
summer; also in shallower water in winter. The eggs are laid in winter. Northern
Europe, and many Irish loughs, but rare
in Britain (notably Ennerdale Water,
Cumbria).

Pontoporeia affinis and opossum
shrimps require water which is not
more than 15°C, but it must be rich
in oxygen. In summer therefore
they can only thrive in a very narrow zone in the lake.

Water Slater *Asellus aquaticus*

Also called Hog-louse. Like aquatic woodlice. Up to
20mm. Flattened and dark brown with light spots,
and long legs and antennae. Female larger than male
and often carries eggs or young in a brood pouch
under her abdomen. Common among rotting leaves
and under stones in woodland ponds and small lakes
and streams and rivers, where it feeds on decaying
plants, algae, carrion etc. Does not swim, but crawls
actively. Tolerates polluted water.

127

Fairy shrimps

Beautiful, graceful and defenceless creatures found in temporary pools (in which their potential predators cannot survive). They do not have a carapace. The head is freely mobile and curves down, and the fairy shrimp swims upside down. They have two pairs of eyes, one pair on stalks, and two pairs of antennae, in males the second is modified as a pair of claspers. Their body is elongated and segmented, and has 11 leaf-shaped pairs of legs with bristles or fine spines at the edges. The abdomen is long and thin. The legs are constantly moving to the rear in waves, propelling the animal forwards. They feed on plankton, especially algae. Females carry the eggs in a sac behind the legs. The eggs can endure frost and require drying in order to hatch. There are five species in Europe, of which only one *(Chirocephalus diaphanus)* is found in Britain.

Siphonophanes grubei

Female up to 25 mm, male up to 22 mm. Orange to dark red. The 11 pairs of legs often have a greenish sheen and move in waves when swimming. The female's 2nd pair of antennae are broad; the male's are long and finger-shaped at the tip and have a large, long, serrated appendage. The female's egg sac, behind the 11th pair of legs is oblong. Feeds on plankton algae and is only found mainly in small drying puddles in woodland and on uncultivated open land; March-May. Not found in Britain or Ireland. In continental Europe, north to Denmark.

A slightly smaller species, *Tanymastix stagnalis*, is widespread in Europe (except the far north) and also occurs in certain Irish pools. The female's 2nd pair of antennae are short; the male's swollen at the base and shaped like two long curved horns. The female's egg sac is short and round.

Tadpole Shrimp
Lepidurus grubei

Body up to 45 mm. Head and large portion of body covered by a large, broad, oval, olive-green to brown carapace with keel and protruding eyes. Segmented body, and the free rearmost segments of the abdomen are dark, almost black. It has two long thin filamentous tails. The 35-50 thoracic feet propel it slowly forward across the bottom. It is a predator, feeding on caddis fly larvae and tadpoles etc. The eggs can endure frost and several years of drying. Found in very few places in small pools and drying ponds, mainly March-May. Non-British.

A similar tadpole shrimp, **Triops cancriformis**, is found throughout Europe, but is very rare in Britain. May-July.

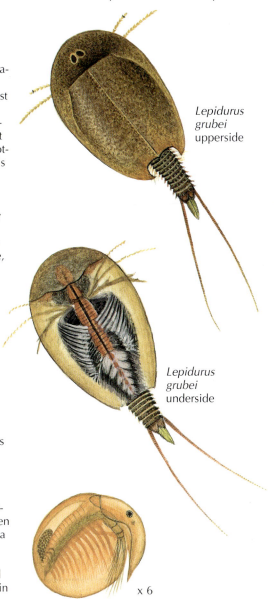

Lepidurus grubei upperside

Lepidurus grubei underside

Clam Shrimp
Lynceus brachyurus

Female up to 6 mm with 12 pairs of legs, male up to 3.9 mm with 10 pairs of legs. Amber. Head covered by a hood-shaped carapace; the female's ends in a point, while the male's is blunt. Body covered by a bivalved, pea-shaped carapace. The female carries the eggs under her shell, and when she dies in autumn, this provides extra protection for the eggs. Feeds on plankton. Rare and found just above the bottom or free-swimming in small drying puddles, May-July. Not found in Britain.

x 6

129

Water fleas

Water fleas have a bivalved transparent shell, covering thorax and abdomen. The head is covered by a hood-shaped shell with a large eye, and the abdomen ends in two claws. The 2nd pair of antennae are long and branched with long bristles, and used for swimming, with rhythmic beats propelling the water flea forward in hops through the water. Most filter-feed on plankton, which is caught by the 4-6 pairs of thoracic limbs and brought forward towards the mouth. A few species feed on carrion, freshwater polyps or are predators. They are found in all types of fresh water, except fast-flowing watercourses.

Bosmina longirostris

Female up to 0.7 mm, male 0.4 mm. Transparent, greyish violet, sometimes bluish or yellowish. Round and rather like a tiny elephant with two very long trunk-like protuberances (first antennae) at tip of head. Male slightly more elongated. Very common in open bodies of water in ponds and lakes; mainly April-October.

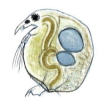

Chydorus sphaericus

Female up to 0.5 mm, male up to 0.4 mm. Colouring varies from pale yellowish green to dark brown. Round or oval and not compressed. No clear separation between head and body carapace. Found in all types of fresh water, except fast-flowing water, especially among plants, but also in plankton in clear-water lakes; March-November.

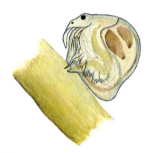

Water fleas make up a large proportion of the food of freshwater polyps (see p. 173-174), which are paralysed by the stinging cells of the tentacles. However, a small round 0.5 mm water flea, **Anchistropus emarginatus**, which is rare, actually feeds on Hydra, which is often destroyed.

Water fleas, which swim freely in the water, change shape during the year. The crest is much longer and more pointed in summer. If the small fish and other predators that primarily feed on water fleas are present in the same body of water as the water fleas, the latter may develop spines on their body, and the terminal spine may grow longer. This is regarded as protection against being eaten.

Daphnia cuculata

Female 1.1-2.5 mm, male 0.8-1.0 mm. Rather transparent. In summer often has bluish or red particulate fat. Compressed body, and long, prickly spine. Found in larger lakes; May-November.

summer   winter

Daphnia pulex

Female up to 3.4 mm, male approx. 1.5 mm. Colouring varies greatly; can be greenish, yellowish, brownish or reddish. Carapace broad and oval and ends in a point. Very common everywhere in ponds, lakes and slow-moving watercourses, and found all year round. However, it is most common April-June and September-October.

Daphnia longispina

Female up to 3 mm, male up to 1.7 mm. Fairly transparent. Colouring varies greatly; may be pale green, reddish or greenish, but is normally yellowish-brown. Body only slightly compressed. Carapace oval, with small spines at the rear. Prickly terminal spine is normally half as long as the animal, but can be longer or shorter. Common everywhere in ponds and in shallow areas of larger lakes; April-November.

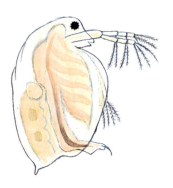

Daphnia magna

Female up to 6 mm, male up to 3 mm. Yellowish, brownish or dirty red. Never clear and transparent, but sometimes the intestine can be seen as a winding tube in the body. Broad and elliptical with a keel on side of carapace, with or without end spine. Relatively small head and long swimming setae. Fairly common in warm, highly-polluted ponds (e.g. village ponds) and small lakes; February-November.

Eurycercus lamellatus

Female up to 4 mm, male up to 1.4 mm. Olive-yellow to olive-brown; in autumn often has bluish or reddish particulate fat. Carapace has keel on back, and head is clearly lower than carapace, which has fairly fine bristles along edge. Found among plants in ponds and lakes and in slow-moving water, and is eaten by many fish, particularly salmonids.

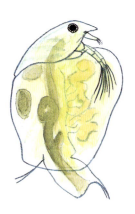

Eurycercus glacialis

Female up to 6 mm, male up to 2 mm. Yellowish to brownish, male lighter, often greyish-white. Seen from the side it is a distorted oval with a high anterior end and a notch where head and body carapace meet. Subarctic cold-water species brought in by migratory birds. Found among plants in dune lakes; April-October.

Water fleas can occur in very large numbers and are often sold in pet shops as live food for aquarium fish.

Sida crystallina

Female up to 4 mm, male up to 1.5 mm. Large and plump, yellowish brown and more or less transparent. Large, triangular head, separated from body by a narrower section. 6 pairs of legs. Male has long 1st antennae. Attachment organs on back of head, used to cling to plants when feeding. Dormant eggs are laid individually. Found among plants in clean ponds and lakes and in rivers with weak currents, April-October.

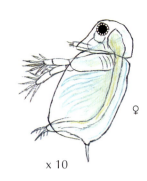

♀

x 10

Ceriodaphnia quadrangula

Female up to 0.9 mm, male up to 0.7 mm. Greyish yellow, transparent with a reddish or greenish sheen, but can be dark brown in acidic, brown-water lakes. Male often slightly darker. Oval, almost round, body. Very long swimming antennae with 9 swimming setae. Curved head with a pronounced rim that in summer may have a spine. Common in clean, acidic large ponds and small to medium lakes, April-November.

Scapholeberis mucronata

Female up to 1.2 mm, male up to 0.8 mm. Blackish brown, often with lighter and darker regions. Slightly compressed, with a large head, and young ones have a forehead horn of variable length. Carapace has a straight rear edge in line with tail spine and with fine setae along edge. The only water flea found hanging upside down in the surface film near the banks of ponds and smaller lakes. It almost skates forward, and feeds on algae and other organic material, which it filters from the surface film. April-November.

Water fleas are important for the recycling of organic substances in ponds and lakes. They eat huge quantities of planktonic algae, break down waste and are in turn food for numerous small aquatic animals and fish.

Iliocryptus sordius

Female approx. 1 mm, male approx. 0.5 mm. Orange when young and dark red when older. Small head. 2nd pair of antennae are thick and powerful with swimming setae. Carapace has a high keel and thick setae at edge. It has 1-9 growth lines: marks from shells moulted as the animal grows. Lives in the mud, primarily in slightly polluted marshes, but also in ponds and lakes, and is often covered by mud. The ephippium (special egg compartment) is not shed by the female.

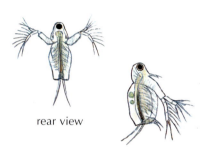

rear view

Diaphanosoma brachyurum

Female up to 1.2 mm, male up to 0.8 mm. Transparent and yellowish. Slender body. Head is separated from body by a deep notch. The swimming antennae are powerful and broad, and one branch has a long, bristle-shaped end that can reach beyond back edge of carapace. It has 6 pairs of legs, swims well and is found in open bodies of water in lakes, but also lives in ponds; May-November. Dormant eggs are laid individually.

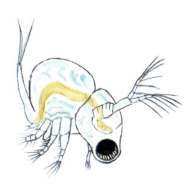

Polyphemus pediculus

A predatory water flea. Female up to 1.8 mm, male up to 1.1 mm. Transparent and yellowish-white. Large head, separated from body by a deep notch and with a large central eye. Carapace does not cover body, but has evolved into a hemispherical brood sac in females. Very short body, and two long steering bristles on abdominal tip. A good and fast swimmer that feeds on smaller crustaceans. Dormant eggs are laid individually. Found locally, primarily among floating leaves and in the outer edge of reed swamps in lakes.

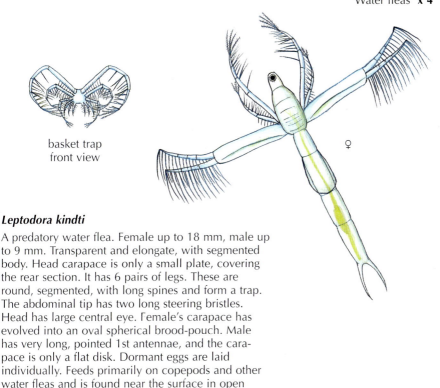

basket trap
front view

♀

Leptodora kindti

A predatory water flea. Female up to 18 mm, male up to 9 mm. Transparent and elongate, with segmented body. Head carapace is only a small plate, covering the rear section. It has 6 pairs of legs. These are round, segmented, with long spines and form a trap. The abdominal tip has two long steering bristles. Head has large central eye. Female's carapace has evolved into an oval spherical brood-pouch. Male has very long, pointed 1st antennae, and the carapace is only a flat disk. Dormant eggs are laid individually. Feeds primarily on copepods and other water fleas and is found near the surface in open water in lakes; June-October.

Water fleas normally reproduce by parthenogenesis (a form of asexual reproduction). Females carry eggs in a brood pouch between the body and carapace. Under certain conditions – such as too many solutes in the water, too little food, a pond drying out, and when the temperature falls in autumn – the smaller males are produced, and they then fertilise the females. These females produce thick-shelled dormant eggs, which can remain unhatched for several years and in many species can withstand desiccation and frost. They are laid either individually or together in part of the mother's carapace, the ephippium. The ephippium often has filaments or barbs that can stick to aquatic birds' feathers. They are also light enough to be dispersed by the wind.

fish louse, seen from the front, from above and from below

Fish Louse
Argulus foliaceus

Female up to 9.5 mm, male up to 8 mm. Greenish on back. Body segments on underside are often orange. Flat like a pancake with a large, broad, round shell on the first body segment, which is fused with the head. The remaining body segments are free. It has four pairs of powerful swimming legs and is a fast swimmer. The eggs, which over-winter, are deposited in rows on aquatic plants and covered by foam. Widespread in summer in nutrient-rich ponds and lakes.

Fish lice are parasites that feed on the blood of fish and amphibians. The antennae and some of the limbs have evolved into a pair of suckers. Other feeding limbs can pierce the host's skin, and can also spray poison into its host, to slow down its movements. A heavy infestation can kill a small fish. These are not true lice, but related to copepods.

Copepods

Copepods are small crustaceans found in two forms, free-living and as parasites. The free-living ones have a simple shell covering the head and front section of the body. The thorax is pear-shaped or oval with five pairs of legs. The abdomen is slender with no legs, but has a pair of bristle-shaped cerci. The first pair of antennae are long, un-branched and used for swimming together with the legs on the thorax. Females carry the eggs in one or two egg sacs, which in the parasitic forms may be very long.

x 20

Canthocamptus sp.

Up to 1 mm. Has fairly short antennae and long cerci. Resembles a silverfish in shape and movement. During mating the male clings on to the female's cerci with its 1st pair of antennae for a long period. Female has only one egg sac. Very commonly found creeping on the bottom or on plants in ditches, puddles, ponds and lakes. May also live in moss and in damp humus in beechwoods.

A similar species, ***Bryocamptus pygmaeus***, is common in wet debris on lake shores.

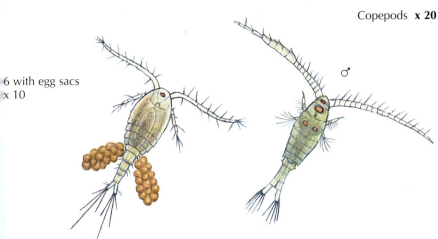

6 with egg sacs
x 10

♂

Cyclops sp.

1-3 mm. Body and antennae brownish. Antennae somewhat curved and shorter than body, which is divided into head/thorax (cephalothorax) and abdomen. The bristles on the cerci are unequal in length. It hops forward in the water by beating with its antennae. Female has two egg sacs. Called after the one-eyed giant of Greek mythology. Very common in ponds and lakes.

Copepod larvae are of the nauplius type. They are short and compressed with only three pairs of limbs. They swim around in the water, but after a short time they change shape, and after moulting about 10 times they become adults.

Diaptomus sp.

1-2 mm. Antennae are as long or longer than body, which is divided into cephalothorax and abdomen. Bristles on cerci are equal in length. Antennae are at right angles to body and keep the copepod vertical in the water, while it swims with its bristle-shaped jaws. Using its four front pairs of legs it can jump upwards in the water. Female has one egg sac. Feeds on plankton algae and is very common in ponds and lakes.

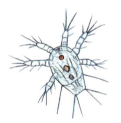

nauplius larva x 50

Copepods often have particulate fat, with bright colouring. They can be found in very large numbers and are an important food for many predatory insects, fish etc.

Copepods can produce dormant eggs like water fleas. However, they can also enclose themselves in a thick-shelled cyst, when conditions become poor, or when the water dries up.

Ostracods

The entire body of an ostracod (or seed shrimp) is covered by a bivalved carapace that functions as a gill and is kept together by an adductor muscle. It is often rather calcified, and so the animals resemble small bivalved molluscs. The carapace can be warty, hairy or smooth, black, green, brown, or white and porcelain-like. Only the antennae, a pair of thoracic limbs and the spiny bipartite abdomen protrude. The swimming forms have large feathery tufts on both pairs of antennae, and they move in jumps through the water. The creeping, bottom-dwelling species have crawling bristles on their antennae, and the second pair have a large claw. Most ostracods are plant eaters and break down rotting leaves etc. Most swimming species feed on plankton. The large ones are predators.

Candona candida

Approx. 1 mm. Porcelain-like white. Very common in ponds and smaller lakes, but can also be found in shallow water in larger lakes.

Cypridopsis vidua

Approx. 0.7 mm. Brown, with long bristles right round edge of carapace. Very common on the surface near the banks of ponds and lakes.

Notodromas monacha

Approx. 1 mm. Black or dark brown. Abdominal edge of carapace is straight and elongated by a spine and has fine hairs and bristles. Clings upside down to the surface film in ponds and lakes.

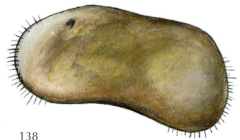

Cypris reptans

Approx. 2.5 mm. Brown, with long bristles at front and back end of carapace. Very common in clear deep water in ponds and lakes. Possibly an ice-age relict.

FRESHWATER COCKLES AND MUSSELS

Freshwater cockles and mussels have two valves that can be closed around the soft parts, two adductors, and some have a few hinge teeth. The valves have more or less distinct growth lines. They feed by filtering the water for algae, bacteria and other small organic material. The large species are unisexual, and produce larvae that parasitise fish for a few weeks. The smaller species produce small but fully-developed offspring.

Pea Mussel
Pisidium sp.

2-6 mm long. Small, thin valves, egg-shaped or rounded triangular. Fine, closely-striped surface, yellowish or greyish horn-coloured. Umbo behind centre. Only one siphon visible in living animals. Long, bluish foot. Common in all types of freshwater, also in drying woodland puddles and brown, acidic lakes lacking in nutrients.
P. casertanum is found primarily in deep water in lakes, *P. amnicum* at the bottom of slow-moving rivers. The eggs develop in brood sacs in the gills. The young mussels are ejected via the siphon.

Acidic lakes lacking in nutrients have a much poorer range of wildlife species than nutrient-rich lakes. Neither mussels nor snails are found in acidic lakes, as there is insufficient calcium in the water for them to construct their houses or shells. Pea mussels are the exception.

Right and left side
The oldest part of a mussel shell often forms a prominent boss, the umbo. Behind it is the hinge ligament. A mussel's right and left side can be identified by placing it upright with the umbo uppermost and pointing forward.

Pisidium amnicum

9-11 mm long. The valves have only a slightly protuberant umbo. Markedly ribbed surface, shiny yellowish grey or greyish brown. Umbo well behind centre. Only one siphon visible in living animals. Found locally in rivers with clayey or sandy bottoms.

Freshwater cockles, orb mussels
Sphaerium corneum

Up to 13 mm long. Extremely convex valves. Central umbo. Two siphons visible in living animals. Common in all types of freshwater. Found primarily among plants near banks of lakes and rivers and in slow-moving outflows from lakes.

Sphaerium lacustre

Up to 9 mm long. Valves with compressed edges, very thin-walled and fragile with narrow, conical central umbo. Two siphons visible in living animals. Found locally in swamps, ditches and small ponds, and in tranquil bays in slow-moving water.

Freshwater cockle, showing two siphons

Pearl Mussel
Margaritana margaritifera

Up to 120 mm long. Adult mussels have very strong, kidney-shaped valves, almost black. Sometimes contain jewel-quality pearls – grains of sand that have been coated with mother-of-pearl. Found in 'soft', i.e. lime-deficient, water on gravelly and stony bottoms. Grow very slowly, reach sexual maturity at age 20 and can live to over 100. Larva parasitises trout and salmon. In Britain in north and west. Possibly a late-glacial cold relict.

x 1

Unio crassus

Up to 79 mm long, but normally 50-60 mm. Solid, heavy valves, oblong, oval with curved upper edge. Powerful hinge with truncated, conical principal teeth in left valve separated by a broad indentation. Dark brown or almost black on outer side; white or salmon-coloured inside. Found locally in continental Europe, in fast-flowing rivers with stony bottoms. Absent from Britain.

Painter's Mussel *Unio pictorum*

Up to 114 mm long, but often smaller. Solid valves with parallel upper and underside. Left valve has two long, almost connected and compressed, sharp principal teeth; the front one is much larger than the rear one. Slender, approx. 2.5 times as long as it is broad. Common in ponds, lakes and rivers, often in fairly deep water, and in tranquil outflows from lakes.

A similar species, **U. tumidus**, has a pointed, egg-shaped valve, and the left valve's two principal teeth are equal in size and only separated by a narrow groove.

young mussel x 3

The large freshwater mussels produce larvae called glochidia. They have 0.4 mm-long, heart-shaped valves and a hook with barbs. They are ejected with exhaled water in April-May and cling to a fish, whose skin grows around them. They parasitise it for 2-3 weeks, after which they burst out as tiny mussels, and the fish rubs them off. They gradually begin living like adults.

Growth rings

The thick rings on a mussel are growth rings. A swan mussel may live as long as 20 years.

Swan Mussel *Anodonta cygnea*

Up to 230 mm long. Thin, fragile valves with a long hinge and no hinge teeth. Bulky, and less than twice as long as it is broad. Common. Largest in lakes, where it slowly ploughs its way through the mud with its foot, often in fairly deep water. Smaller in watercourses, where it often remains immobile, e.g. in slow-moving outflows from lakes. Several subspecies.

young mussel

A mussel can creep forward on the bottom using its foot. The foot protrudes and the tip grips. By drawing in its foot the mussel pulls itself forward. Swan Mussels make long ploughed furrows behind them in this way in shallow water on lake beds.

Zebra Mussel
Dreissena polymorpha

Up to 30 mm long, but in rare cases can be larger. Triangular valves with dark bands and a toothless hinge. Resembles marine mussel in shape. Rests attached to the bottom, stones, posts etc. by 100-200 byssus threads. Spread from eastern Europe, to west and north, including Britain, where locally common in lakes, rivers and canals. The eggs are ejected in clutches, and develop into free-swimming larvae in late spring. After 2-3 weeks they sink to the bottom and begin living like adults.

FRESHWATER SNAILS

Operculate snails (snails with a lid)
Operculate snails have gills in front of the heart. They all have a spirally-coiled shell and a lid, the operculum, on the back of the foot. This lid closes the opening when the snail retracts itself into its shell. All species have a dextral shell. Almost all are unisexual, i.e. there are both males and females. They usually live on the bottom or partially buried.

River Snail, Freshwater Winkle
Viviparus fasciatus

35-50 mm high, 25-38 mm across. Olive green or brownish, with three more or less distinct spiral bands. 6-7 bulging whorls divided by a deep suture, and with a broad umbilicus. Dark greyish or brownish body, with lighter foot and numerous small red or yellow spots on the upperside. Occurs locally, particularly in ponds and ditches, but also in streams and lakes, on both stony and muddy bottoms. Easily overlooked, as it often lives buried in the mud. Feeds primarily on detritus. Gives birth to live young. There can be up to 50 young of various sizes in one female in the summer.
The shell of a newborn snail is approx. 7 mm across and has 2-3 spiral bands with bristles. A similar species **V. viviparus**, height 26-30 mm, has an inconspicuous umbilicus, shallow suture and flatter whorls.

A dextral shell has the aperture to the right of the central axis when it is held upright with the aperture facing the observer.

Columella

In the middle of a snail's shell is a column running from top to bottom, the columella, around which the shell winds itself. This may be solid or hollow, and in some snails opens at the umbilicus beside the shell aperture.

Nerite *Theodoxus fluviatilis*

5-8 mm high, 7-10 mm across. Shell is thick, broad and smooth with a small spire and two small whorls. White-speckled like a chessboard and varying greatly in colour, but it cannot be confused with other snails. Occurs locally on stones by shores of large lakes, also on stones in rivers and in brackish water, where the shell is often black. Lid is often orange. Feeds on plants and detritus.

Eggs are laid in small round capsules approx. 1 mm in size on stones, plants and shells of other animals. Each capsule contains approx. 80 eggs, but only one larva emerges, as the first to develop eats the others.

x 3

Measuring snails

Height is measured from the outer edge of the shell aperture to the tip along the shell axis. Width is measured from the outer edge of the shell aperture to the edge of the broadest whorl. Whorls are counted from the top out towards the shell aperture.

Valve snails have a feather-like gill, which can occasionally be seen protruding from the shell aperture when the snail is undistured.

Valvata cristata

1-1.3 mm high, 2.5-3.5 mm across. Disc-shaped shell, with open umbilicus, completely flat spire and circular aperture. 3-5 whorls with deep suture. Light or dark horn-colour, but often with a dark covering. Can be confused with small ramshorn snails, but has a lid and a circular aperture. Lid is horny, with dense spiral rings. Common in ponds and lakes, but also found in rivers.

Valvata piscinalis

4-8 mm high, 5-6 mm across. Shell broadly conical, with 4-5 round or slightly flattened whorls. Circular aperture. Umbilicus narrow, occasionally closed. Common in lakes, sometimes in deep water, but found also in rivers.

x 6

Spire Shell
Potamopyrgus (Hydrobia)

4-5 mm high, 2.5-3 mm across. Conical, pointed shell with approx. 6 bulging whorls, deep suture, no umbilicus and with an oval aperture. Spirally-coiled lid. Light horn-colour, but generally has a dark, almost black covering. Common in brackish water, and can appear in enormous numbers. Has moved into fresh water in many areas.

x 10

Marstoniopsis (Bythinella) scholtzi

2.5-3.5 mm high, 1.5-1.9 mm across. Small shell, almost spherical, turret-shaped, has 4-5 bulging whorls with deep suture, narrow umbilicus and egg-shaped aperture. Rare, but found primarily in large lakes and rivers. Local in north-west England and Scotland.

Bithynia leachii

5-8 mm high, 4-6 mm across. Conical shell has 4-5 extremely bulging, step-like whorls, deep suture and oval aperture. Light or dark horn-colour. Calcified lid is not pointed and cannot be pulled into the shell of the fully-grown snail. Common in lakes and slow-flowing rivers.

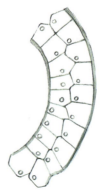

egg mass

x 5

Common Bithynia
Bithynia tentaculata

9-12 mm high, 6-8 mm across. Conical
shell, with 5-6 fairly flat whorls and shallow suture. Aperture pointed at the top.
Light or dark horn-colour, occasionally
with a reddish or greenish sheen. Pointed, pear-shaped lid, thin and horny, with
spiral rings. Very common in ponds,
lakes and rivers. Often found on stones
in the splash zone of lakes, occasionally
in very deep water. A slow and sluggish
animal that can sit still for days.
Eggs are laid in 10-15 mm long capsules
on stones and on other snails' shells,
where the approx. 50 eggs lie in two or
three rows.
Occasionally the red head of a non-
biting midge larva can be seen sticking
out of the shell aperture. This insect usually only uses the snail for protection and
as a means of transport, but it will occasionally devour its host and pupate in the
shell.

sweet
flag

Pulmonate snails

Pulmonate snails have no gills, but breathe through their skin and using a kind of lung. Shell shape varies widely but is usually spirally coiled, and there is no lid for closing up the aperture. Most have dextral shells. Pulmonate snails are hermaphrodite, each individual being both male and female. Almost all are found on aquatic plants or hanging beneath the water's surface.

Moss Bladder Snail
Aplexa hypnorum

12-15 mm high, 4-5 mm across. Thin, sinistral shell is tall and spindle-shaped, with 6 flat whorls, of which the largest comprises half the entire height of the shell. Shell is very shiny, smooth and horn-brown; snail is blue-black. More mobile than other freshwater snails and can do a kind of jump by flinging the shell powerfully to the side. Occurs locally in drying woodland ditches and occasionally in spring puddles.

Dwarf Pond Snail
Lymnaea truncatula

8-10 mm high, 4-5 mm across. Conical shell, with 5-6 extremely bulging whorls, step-like and marked by a deep suture. Umbilicus is narrow, like a crack. Brown. Common in ditches, flooded meadows, dried-out puddles, small ponds and streams, particularly on the margin between land and water.
Intermediate host for the Large Liver-fluke, Fasciola hepatica, 3-4 cm, found in the livers of sheep and cattle.

Mud Snail
Lymnaea glabra

14-16 mm high, 4.5-5.5 mm across. Turret-shaped shell twice as high as its small aperture, with 7-8 flat or slightly bulging whorls. Yellowish horn-coloured. Found mainly in ponds and ditches, including those which dry out regularly.

Marsh Snail
Lymnaea palustris

15-25 mm high, 7-11 mm across. Fairly solid shell, pointed and conical, with fairly deep suture. 6-7 coarsely-striped, slightly bulging whorls, with no umbilicus. Spire only slightly higher than elongated egg-shaped aperture. Usually dark horn-brown. Very common in ditches and ponds, but also found in lakes and rivers.

Great Pond Snail
Lymnaea stagnalis

50-60 mm high, 25-30 mm across. Thin shell has high, slender spire, with 6-8 compressed whorls. Last whorl is large and fat, with an egg-shaped aperture. Yellowish horn-coloured, finely striped. Common in ponds and lakes with abundant plant life, particularly at the surface.
Very large egg capsules, 5-6 cm long, can contain up to approx. 300 eggs.

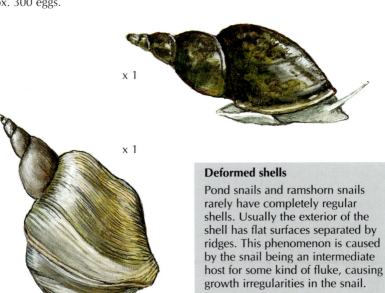

x 1

x 1

Deformed shells

Pond snails and ramshorn snails rarely have completely regular shells. Usually the exterior of the shell has flat surfaces separated by ridges. This phenomenon is caused by the snail being an intermediate host for some kind of fluke, causing growth irregularities in the snail.

149

Ear Snail
Lymnaea auricularia

24-32 mm high, 20-25 mm across. Shell resembles that of Wandering Snail, but has a narrow, pointed spire. 4-5 whorls, the last very large and fat. Suture quite flat. Aperture large and ear-like. Common in clumps of reeds in ponds and small lakes, and in slow-flowing waters.

Wandering Snail
Lymnaea peregra

15-20 mm high, 10-14 mm across. Shell resembles that of Ear Snail, but has a low, blunt spire. 4-5 whorls, the last large and fat. Suture quite deep, umbilicus completely or almost completely closed. Aperture large and egg-shaped, somewhat pointed. Common in clumps of reeds in ponds, lakes, streams and rivers with abundant plant life. Varies greatly and can be substantially larger in some lakes. Can be found in large numbers in polluted watercourses.

Bladder Snail
Physa fontinalis

9-11 mm high, 6-8 mm across. Sinistral, translucent shell is thin and delicate, fat and egg-shaped. Spire is low and truncated. Shell is light horn-coloured and usually fairly shiny. Aperture is elongated and egg-shaped, pointed at the top, taking up 2/3 of the snail's height. Mantle edge has lobes that wrap around the shell in oxygen-deficient water. Creeps very rapidly and can do a kind of jump by flinging its shell powerfully to the side. Common in ponds, lakes and rivers, often found in deep water, even in eutrophic conditions.

x 3

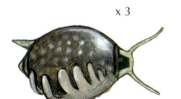

Succinea putris

15-22 mm high, 7-12 mm across. Thin, translucent shell is shiny and golden-brown, with 3-4 whorls. Last whorl is large and fat. Egg-shaped aperture, pointed, 2/3 of snail's height. Resembles a pond snail, but spire is lower. A land snail, common on sweet-grass and other plants near lakes and rivers, occasionally submerged.

Succinea putris is the intermediate host for a fluke, *Leucochloridium macrostomum*, 2 mm in length. Its green or yellow club-shaped embryo sacs can be seen in the snail's distended antennae. These eventually take the form of 1 cm long, striped mobile worms, which get eaten by birds such as robins and wagtails. The adult fluke then lives in the bird's gut.

x 3

Glutinous Snail
Myxas glutinosa

13-22 mm high, 10-20 mm across. Very thin, translucent shell, almost spherical, with a very small spire. When the snail is alive the shell is almost completely covered by the mantle. Rare, found in ponds, lakes and rivers with dense plant growth.

Ramshorn snails

Ramshorn snails are pulmonates. Their shells do not have a point, but are spirally coiled, making them resemble a flat disc, thinnest in the centre. Most have red blood.

Planorbis contortus

1.5-2 mm high, 5-6.5 mm across. Dull, opaque shell has 7-8 high whorls with a deep suture, a bulging underside and no keel. Underside bulging, with broad, umbilicus-like hollow. Brownish, finely striped. Very common in ponds, lakes and slow-moving rivers.

Planorbis leucostoma

1.2-1.3 mm high, 7-8 mm across. Yellowish or brownish shell, faintly shiny and finely striped. 6-7 low whorls, flat on the underside, with distinct right-angled edge up to the bowed upper-side; no keel. Common in springs, ponds and streams.

seen from beneath x 3

Planorbis vortex

1-1.2 mm high, 9-11 mm across. Translucent shell rather thin and delicate, light horn-coloured and shiny. 6-7 whorls. Flat on the underside; bulging on the upperside and slightly under the centre. Slight keel. Common in ponds, lakes and slow-moving rivers. Occasionally spotted drifting on the water surface in summer.

Planorbis albus

Approx. 1.5 mm high, 5-6 mm across.
Dull, opaque shell, yellowish or light
grey-green, often very light. 3.5-5
whorls with transverse lines, crossed
by many spiral lines. No keel. Extended aperture. Common in ponds, lakes
and rivers with abundant plant life,
often in quite deep water. A similar
species, **P. laevis**, has a very shiny
shell; it is uncommon.

P. laevis

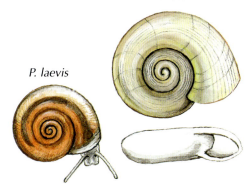

Planorbis crista

Approx. 0.5 mm high, approx. 3 mm across. Lens-
shaped shell is horn-coloured, often with a dark
covering, finely striped, often with transverse furrows.
3-4 whorls, greatly extended at the aperture and with
a centrally-positioned keel. Common in ponds and
small lakes. Unlike other ramshorn snails it never
comes to the surface to breathe.

x 10

Segmentina nitida

1.5-1.7 mm high, 5-6 mm across. Shiny lens-shaped
shell is translucent orange or red-brown. Flat underside, bulging upperside, 4 whorls; interior has lamellae, visible when shell is held up to the light and as
white marks on the exterior. Rather uncommon in
Britain. In ponds with abundant plant life; occasionally also in springs, and more rarely in large lakes and
rivers.

Segmentina complanata

Approx. 2 mm high, 6-7 mm across. Lens-shaped
shell is shiny and translucent. 4-5 sharp-edged
whorls; no internal lamellae. Common in ponds with
abundant plant life, and more rarely, in large lakes
and rivers.

x 1.5

Great Ramshorn Snail
Planorbarius corneus

12-16 mm high, 25-37 mm across. Large, thick shell, almost half as high as it is broad, slightly sunken in the centre on both sides. 5-6 rounded, irregularly striped whorls. Light or dark olive brown upperside. Light yellowish underside. Common in ponds and small lakes with abundant plant growth, but also found in large lakes and slow-moving rivers.
Eggs are laid in oval egg capsules, which can be as large as 3 cm in diameter, containing approx. 70 eggs.

Common Ramshorn Snail
Planorbis planorbis

3.5-4 mm high, 15-22 mm across. Rather solid shell is brown, occasionally almost black.5.5-6 whorls with thread-like keel near the underside. Suture deep on the upperside, flatter on the underside. Very common in ponds and small lakes with abundant plant life, and also found in rivers.

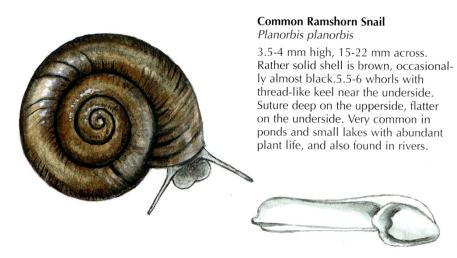

Keeled Ramshorn Snail
Planorbis carinatus

2.5-3.2 mm high, 14-18 mm across. Thin-walled shell is yellowish, rather shiny and finely striped; not lens-shaped. 4.5-5 slightly bulging whorls; sharp central keel. Common in ponds and lakes, especially with clean water.

River Limpet
Ancylus fluviatilis

3 mm high, 5 mm across, 6 mm long. Thin-walled shell is high and cap-shaped, with a broad, egg-shaped aperture, broadest at the front. Has an extremely large foot in relation to its size. Common on stony bottoms in fast-flowing water, normally sitting in such a way that the top of its 'cap' turns away from the current. Also found in the splash zone of lakes with sandy, stony bottoms. Moves very little and never comes to the surface to breathe.

Egg mass of River Limpet

Lake Limpet
Acroloxus lacustris

1.6 mm high, 3.5 mm across, 7 mm long. Thin horn-coloured shell is almost clear, and has the shape of a shallow shield, with almost parallel sides. Tip is clearly to left of centre; aperture is elongated. Resembles a small brown scale or shield. Common in clumps of reeds, on leaves and twigs in ponds and lakes, but can also be found in sections of large, slow-moving rivers. Never breathes at the surface, breathing instead through the skin in a section of the mantle modified as a gill.

FLUKES

Flukes are parasitic flatworms that closely resemble turbellaria but have one or two large suckers. They are divided into two classes:
Monogenea flukes only have one host and are external parasites, usually on the gills or skin of fish.
Digenea flukes have one or more intermediate hosts, where the larvae develop. Adults are internal parasites on warm-blooded vertebrates, particularly mammals and birds, normally in the intestine, but also in veins.

Diplozoon paradoxum

A gill-fluke. 6-10 mm. Often joined in an X shape. Found primarily on the gills of cyprinids.

x 24

Gyrodactylus elegans

A gill-fluke. Approx. 0.7 mm. Viviparous. Parasite on the gills and skin of cyprinids and salmonids which can make them seriously ill.

Digenea flukes have a complex life cycle. The adult flukes discharge around 100,000 eggs, which are released with the faeces. In the water they develop into larvae, miracidia. These are only 0.1 mm long, and bore their way into an intermediate host, usually a snail, but can also be found in mussels. The larva develops into a sac-shaped body, a sporocyst. Sporocysts feed on blood and develop into as many as several hundred more sporocysts, which distribute themselves in the intermediate host's body. These then develop into a new parasitic form, redia larvae, which feed on the intermediate host's tissue. Each redia larva generates up to 1,000 of the fluke's third larval form, cercariae, which have a body with two suckers and a tail. The cercariae bore their way out of the intermediate host and live as plankton in ponds and lakes. They must enter the principal host in one or two days, either by boring their way through the skin or by being eaten. If boring in they lose their tail and only the body develops into an adult.
Some cercariae bore their way into another intermediate host for transport. This is often an insect, e.g. a mosquito larva. Once this has been eaten by the principal host, their development continues.

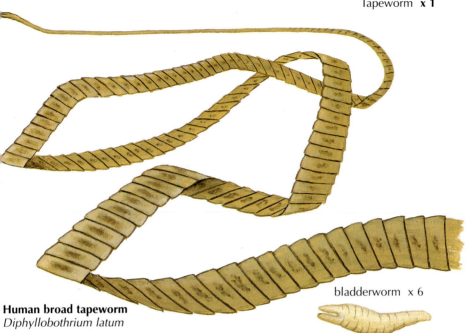

bladderworm x 6

Human broad tapeworm
Diphyllobothrium latum

Up to 20 m long, but rarely longer than a few metres. Grey or brownish and can consist of several thousand segments, which are 10-15 mm wide and 3-5 mm long. The head is 2-3 mm long with two long suckers. Lives in the small intestine of humans and other fish-eating mammals. A medium-sized worm can lay up to 1 million eggs a day. If these end up in fresh water, they will hatch. The first larval stage is free-living. If the larvae are eaten by copepods (of the genera *Cyclops* or *Diaptomus*), they develop into the second larval stage in the body cavity. If infected copepods are eaten by a fish, they develop into the third larval stage, which is 1-2 cm long, white and featureless. The larvae migrate into the fish's flesh, surrounded by hard tissue and become bladderworms. If the fish is eaten uncooked by the end host, the fully-grown tapeworm develops in the intestine. Found mainly in Norway, Sweden and Finland.

The broad tapeworm can be dangerous, as it absorbs large amounts of vitamin B12 from its host, sometimes causing anaemia. This can result in the death of the host.

The broad tapeworm's larvae are transferred to humans, if the fish is eaten raw or poorly prepared. Larvae in fish flesh are killed by deep freezing or by thorough cooking.

TURBELLARIA

Turbellaria are flatworms that are densely covered with fairly small hairs, cilia. The microturbellaria swim by moving these hairs. The larger turbellaria (triclads/planarians) creep along like snails on a mucous layer. The slime is poisonous to fish, and thus prevents them being eaten. They are predators, catching rotifers, small crustaceans, small worms and other turbellaria with the help of their slime. The mouth is roughly in the centre of the abdomen. The branched intestine is visible in some of the larger species. They have no anus and indigestible remnants are spat out through the mouth. All species are hermaphrodite, but they can also reproduce asexually. The eggs, which are sometimes visible inside the animals, are laid in round cocoons, sometimes on stalks, on aquatic plants.

turbellarian of the genus *Neorhabdocoela*

Dalyella viridis

Up to 5 mm. Colourless or green. The green colouring is caused by unicellular green algae that it eats, and which survive and reproduce in the skin. Brown eggs sometimes visible inside its body. Common in spring in drying puddles, primarily in marshes.

Although turbellaria have eyes, they cannot see very much. They orient themselves mainly by detecting dark and light.

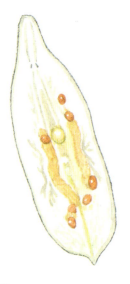

Mesostoma ehrenbergi

Up to 15 mm. Very transparent. Hangs from the surface film by a mucus thread and catches water fleas and other small animals by doubling up into a 'basket trap'. In summer it carries thin-shelled eggs inside it, or larvae that gradually bore their way out through the skin. In autumn thick-shelled eggs can be seen, which are released when the animal dies. Common in lakes with abundant plant life, but difficult to spot. A similar species, which is not so common, **M. craci**, up to 13 mm, is a beautiful cherry-red and found only in spring puddles that dry up in summer.

Crenobia alpina

Up to 10 mm. Slate-grey to black or dark brown. Head has two close-set eyes and two 'horns'. Reproduces by fission in summer, but by sexual reproduction in winter. Rather local in cold springs and cold, upland streams. It can survive subterranean waters. Possibly a late-glacial cold relict.

Phagocata vitta

Up to 8 mm. Whitish to grey. Blunt, rounded head with two close-set eyes positioned a long way back. Found locally in springs and fast-flowing cold streams.

x 2

Dendrocoelum lacteum

Up to 2 mm. Pale milky white to grey. Slightly developed 'front corners' on head. Two black eyes at front set far apart. Distinct intestine. After reciprocal mating a round egg cocoon is formed, in which approx. 40 young develop. The cocoon is forced out through the skin. A predator that also eats carrion and fish eggs. Very common in all types of fresh water, often under stones in lake splash zones.

egg cocoon on beech leaf x 2

Polycelis felina

Up to 7 mm. Brownish on back, lighter on belly. Two 'horns' on head. Eyes in a row along edge of forepart of body. Found only in running water and cold springs. Possibly a late-glacial cold relict.

egg
cocoon

Polycelis nigra/tenuis

Up to 12 mm. Two species that are almost impossible to tell apart by appearance. Dark brown or black. Eyes in a row along edge of front of body. *P. tenuis* often has yellowish or darker longitudinal stripes, while *P. nigra* is often more uniformly dark brown. Very common in all types of fresh water.

Dugesia gonocephala

Up to 20 mm. Brownish to greyish black on upperside. Fairly active. Head distinctly triangular. Equal distance between the two eyes and from each eye out to nearest edge of head. Common in running water in continental Europe, but absent from Britain.

Dugesia lugubris/polychroa

Up to 20 mm. Two very similar species, difficult to distinguish. Brown to black. Blunt triangular head with two light lines. Gap between eyes is greater than distance between eyes and nearest edge of head. The egg cocoons are deposited on stalks on aquatic plants. Common in lakes, streams and rivers.

> Turbellaria break apart easily and have the ability to regenerate. Even a small section can develop into a new animal, and they are therefore easy to clone.

Bdellocephala punctata

Largest European flatworm, up to 35 mm. Brown or yellowish with dark spots. Anterior end has 'neck' and smaller lobes. Sides of body are often wavy. Found locally in rivers, lakes and canals, often under stones in shallow water.

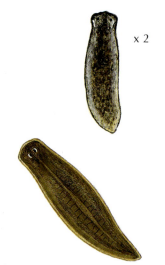

x 2

egg cocoon

Planaria torva

Up to 15 mm. Dark on back, slate-grey to brown, lighter on belly. Head rather square. Two close-set black eyes. Found locally in lakes.

LEECHES

Leeches are annelids with 33 segments, which are divided up into several narrow rings, and have no bristles. They often have a small sucker at the anterior end and a larger one at the posterior end. Most have eyespots. They are hermaphrodite. In the mating season a swelling forms slightly ahead of centre of body, a saddle, a clitellum, which is familiar from other segmented worms, e.g. earthworms. The eggs are laid in cocoons on plants and stones or in the ground, or carried under the belly. Leeches are found in shallow water. They are predators that swallow their prey whole, suck it dry or attach themselves to a host animal as parasites. There are three sub-orders involved: fish leeches and relatives (rhynchobdellids); jawed leeches (gnathobdellids); swallowing leeches (pharyngobdellids).

Fish leeches and their relatives

These have a muscular proboscis that can stretch out and bore into the prey. They are bloodsuckers. Their own blood is colourless. There are two groups: glossiphonids and fish leeches.

Glossiphonids

Glossiphonids are flat, egg-shaped or oblong and oval. They are firm and rubbery to the touch and often roll up into a ball if disturbed. The eggs are laid in thin sac-like capsules, which the adult watches over or carries under its belly. The young also remain here until they can survive by themselves.

Theromyzon tessulatum

Up to 10 cm long and a few cm wide. Greyish green or dark olive-green with longitudinal rows of yellow spots. Soft, gelatinous, almost transparent body with four pairs of eyes in two parallel rows. Common in ponds, lakes and slow-moving rivers. Lies in wait on aquatic plants for grubbing ducks, geese, coots etc., grips the nose and slips into the nasal cavity or throat, where it sucks the blood. A duck with 3-4 blood-sucking leeches in its throat can be choked and may die. The young (200-300) emerge from the cocoon June-July. They leave the parent when they are approx. 1 cm long.

Glossiphonia concolor

Up to 25 mm, grey to light brown with two rows of intermittent lines on its back, that may continue right down to posterior end on belly. Back also has brown and yellow spots. 2-3 pairs of eyes in two parallel rows. Feeds on snails and is found on stones near banks of lakes and rivers. Lays its eggs slightly earlier than *G. complanata*.

adult with young

Glossiphonia heteroclita

Up to 15 mm, found in a light and dark form. The front pair of eyes are closer set than the back two pairs, which may often be merged. Feeds primarily on snails. Common on plants in ponds and lakes. Mating season is June-October, and both egg cocoons and the greenish-blue young are carried under the parent's belly.

Glossiphonia complanata

Up to 30 mm, with two rows of blackish-brown lines on back, interrupted by papillae. Also speckled with yellow and dark-brown small spots; underside is pale. It has three pairs of eyes, in two parallel rows on the head. Feeds primarily on snails. Very common on stones near banks of lakes and rivers, but also found in ponds and streams. Lays eggs in May in cocoons on stones, which adult watches over. One week later the young emerge, approx. 30, and remain attached under the adult for three weeks.

Hemiclepsis marginata

Up to 30 mm. Head and front sucker are clearly separate from body, which is firm and opaque. Green or pale yellow with longitudinal rows of lemon-yellow spots down its back. Head has two pairs of eyes; rear pair distinctly larger than front pair. Feeds primarily on blood of fish, but also attacks amphibians. Common in ponds and lakes with abundant plant life and in slow-moving water.
Breeding season June-August; approx. 50 yellow or green eggs.

Helobdella stagnalis

Up to 10 mm. Greenish on back and lighter on belly. Easily recognisable by the small, dark, hardened scale on its back behind its two eyes. Feeds primarily on midge larvae, water slaters and ramshorn snails. Very common in ponds, lakes and rivers, and can be found in polluted water. Eggs produced May-August. Young can be found June-September. Larger young under the parent's belly feed with the adult.

When a shadow falls across a leech, it may be from an animal moving above it. Those species that do not suck blood will often go flat and rigid. The blood-sucking leeches, however, will move up through the water following the shadow.

Fish leeches

Fish leeches are long, slender and round rhynchobdellids with a large, round, parabolic sucker, clearly distinct from body at both anterior and posterior end. They suck blood from fish, and show no parental care.

Piscicola geometra

Up to 80 mm. Slender, not very contractile leech. Almost cylindrical in cross section. Front sucker has two pairs of eyes, and along rim of large rear sucker are 12-14 small pinpoint-sized eyespots. Beautifully patterned in dark green and white, and has small vesicles along body that act as gills. Normally rests like a rigid stick on aquatic plants on its rear sucker, but will swim rapidly towards fish that come near. Found primarily among plants in lakes and rivers. Young are free-swimming from the first. Eggs are laid individually in 1-1.5mm-long brown cocoons, April-July.

egg cocoons

egg cocoon x 10

Jawed leeches

Jawed leeches (gnathobdellids) have three powerful jaws with sharp teeth along the edge and 10 eyes in a curve along edge of anterior end. Their blood is red. Eggs are laid in a large cocoon on land in damp soil. They undertake no parental care.

Medicinal Leech
Hirudo medicinalis

Up to 15 cm. Large and powerful, dark green on back with 6 orange or brown longitudinal bands, usually interrupted by black spots. Underside dark grey and marbled. Rear sucker is almost as wide as body.
Breeds in July. Cocoon, up to 3 cm long, can hold 15 eggs. After approx. two months the young creep out and down to the water. Can live for more than 15 years.

Leeches do not like salt. So if a Medicinal Leech has attached itself to the skin to suck blood, simply sprinkle a little salt on it to make it let go.

Leeches move like inchworms, by stretching their front end forward, taking a grip and then drawing their rear end up to their head. Jawed leeches and swallowing leeches can swim by moving their bodies sinuously up and down.

When small, Medicinal Leeches suck blood from worms, snails, fish and frogs. Larger ones prefer the blood of mammals, including people. One meal increases the leech's weight 5-10 times. It sucks 10-15 cm^3 blood and prevents it coagulating with the substance hirudin in its saliva. It prefers to have one meal per year, but the extracted blood can stay fresh for 1 year in the leech.
Medicinal Leeches were formerly used for blood-letting, and they have been over-collected for this and for research. They are also threatened by habitat loss and now enjoy protected status. In Britain this species is very local, found notably in marshy pools at Dungeness. The bite of the Medicinal Leech is surprisingly painless. If you cut the rear tip of the animal off, it may still persist in sucking blood. The sucking leech can be removed with the fingers, but the blood will continue to flow until the anti-coagulant saliva has been washed out.

Horse Leech
Haemopis sanguisuga

Up to 15 cm. Back is uniform dark green to brownish black, sometimes with a regular pattern of greyish-brown longitudinal stripes. Belly is uniform light grey or greenish-yellow. Feeds on smaller animals such as square-tailed worms, midge larvae, snails etc. Sometimes crawls on land after earthworms. Common under stones near the banks of lakes, but found most frequently in ditches and ponds, often just under the water surface.

Breeding season July-August. The cocoon, up to 19 mm long, can hold 16 eggs. The young that emerge are approx. 15 mm long.

Horse Leeches, despite their name, do not attack horses, or any other mammal, and cannot penetrate mammalian skin.

Most leeches avoid light, hiding among plants or under stones. *Theromyzon tessulatum, Hemiclepsis marginata* and Medicinal Leech, which are all bloodsuckers, are attracted to light. *Theromyzon tessulatum* and Medicinal Leech, which suck blood from warm-blooded animals, are also attracted by heat.

Leeches have a well-developed chemical sense. If you add fluid from a pond snail to a bowl of glossiphonid leeches, for example, they will immediately begin making searching movements. A stick rubbed against a fish and stuck down into the water close to a fish leech will immediately be attacked by it. *Theromyzon tessulatum* will react in the same way to a stick rubbed against the preen gland of a duck, and medicinal leeches to a stick rubbed in human sweat.

egg cocoons x 6

Swallowing leeches

Swallowing leeches have neither proboscis nor jaws, and swallow their prey. They have 8 eyes, in pairs in two transverse rows on the head. Their blood is red, and they undertake no parental care.

Erpobdella octoculata

Up to 6 cm. Slender and brownish with a network of black spots on back and light transverse stripes, but can also be almost completely devoid of spots and stripes. Found in almost all types of fresh water. Feeds on worms, midge larvae, small crustaceans, smaller leeches etc., which are swallowed whole.

The eggs, up to 20, are laid in cocoons, up to 9 mm long, May-October on stones and aquatic plants. They are brownish, thick-shelled, oval and lemon-shaped with a point at either end.

Erpobdella testacea

Up to 5 cm. Normally plain brownish and almost transparent, but can have a broad dark band down along its back. Common in ponds, lakes and slow-moving rivers. Feeds as *E. octoculata*, but its egg cocoons are not pointed.

Dina lineata

Slender leech, up to 5 cm. Brown or greyish, with four narrow dark longitudinal bands down its back and a light central stripe. Feeds as *Erpobdella octoculata*. In Britain mainly northern.

Lays its eggs (3-4) in July in 4mm-long plump cocoons with a point at both ends.

SEGMENTED WORMS

Segmented worms have a few microscopic bristles that generally stick straight out of the skin. They are hermaphrodite, and sexually-mature animals form a saddle-like thickening of skin at their centre, a clitellum. This contains a mass of glands and is used during mating. The saddle is also used for forming the cocoon, for the eggs. Worms live either buried in the ground or crawling in algae and detritus on the bottom and on stones. However, a number of them can swim. Some are pale or transparent; others are red or brownish, as they have haemoglobin in their blood, and they can therefore live in very oxygen-deficient water. Worms may thus be the only animals found on the bottom of deep lakes and in very polluted waters.

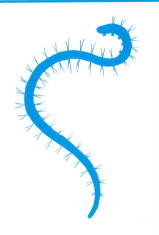

Naididae

Fairly small worms, most less than 2 cm long. They often have two eyes and a fairly transparent body. The bristles are in bunches, a few on the underside and a few on the upperside of each segment. However, there are rarely any bristles on the upperside of the foremost segment. Most species have eyespots at the anterior end. Naidids normally lack haemoglobin in their blood, and the few species that have it are never as bright red as worms such as Tubifex. Some can swim; others crawl on the bottom. They never twist themselves into a ball when disturbed. Reproduction is mainly asexual, and they divide by budding, initially forming chains of two or three individuals. Sexually mature specimens are found primarily in autumn, when you can also find their egg cocoons, which only hold 1 egg.

Dero **sp.**

2.5-15 mm. Lacks eyes, but has four small finger-like red anal gills. Bristles on back from 4th or 6th segment. Lives in clear, slightly yellowish slime tubes, but can swim. Common on plants at the bottom of ponds and lakes.

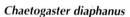

Chaetogaster diaphanus

Approx. 15 mm. Transparent and fairly chunky. No eyes and only has bristles on underside. Very long, hooked bristles in bunches of 6-13. Predator that feeds on rotifers, small water fleas, mosquito larvae and other worms. Large mouth, and swallows prey whole. The prey may be clearly visible swimming round inside the intestinal tract for a while, until the stomach acids kill it. Common in pure, clear water on aquatic plants and algae-covered stones in ponds, lakes and rivers.

Chaetogaster limnaei

1-5 mm. Whitish, lacks eyes and only has bristles on underside. Hooked bristles in bunches. Feeds partially parasitically on snails infected by flukes, particularly great pond snail and ramshorn snails. They can be seen as small fringes around the shell orifice, on the foot and the antennae and feed on hatching cercariae. There may be more than 1,000 of them on a single snail. Found locally in ponds and lakes, and in slow rivers.

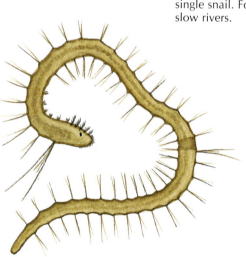

Slavina appendiculata

2-20 mm. Brown and opaque, as it is surrounded by a sheath of mud. Has eyes. Hair bristles on 6th segment are very long. Crawls on bottom in lakes and rivers.

Stylaria lacustris

5.5-18 mm. Has a long proboscis and long bristles. Bunches of 1-3 hair bristles and 3-4 hooked bristles on back. Hooked bristles on underside are jointed. Swims on its side with fast horizontal body movements. Common among plants near banks in ponds, lakes and rivers and can be found in large numbers.

view of back

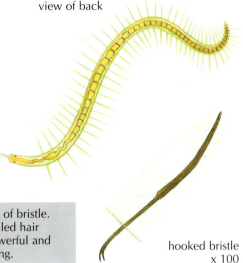

Segmented worms have several kinds of bristle. The slender, pointed filaments are called hair bristles. Hooked bristles are more powerful and usually have an upper and lower prong.

hooked bristle
x 100

Ripistes parasita

2-7.5 mm. Has proboscis. Front section of body is reddish or yellowish-brown. Front hair bristles on upperside are very long. Swims almost perpendicular in the water, but often rests with its posterior end in a transparent tube. Anterior end is free and moves up and down in a rhythmic movement. The hair bristles are sticky and collect small algae and detritus, which the animal licks up. Found locally, primarily on water-lilies in ponds and small acidic lakes.

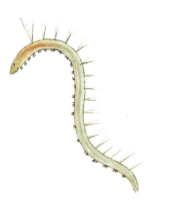

Nais sp.

2-12 mm. Normally has eyes. Front segment reddish-brown. Hair bristles much longer than hooked bristles, and in bunches of 1-5. Active and swims a lot. In summer often seen with a tail of small individuals attached to its rear. Feeds on plants, primarily diatoms. Common among plants in lakes and rivers.

N. elinguis is often found in large numbers in organically-polluted waters.

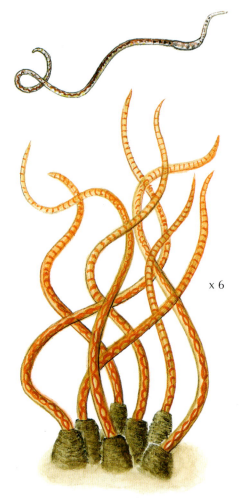

Tubifex tubifex

A sludge worm. 30-40 mm. Red due to the haemoglobin in its blood. Lives in slime tubes at the bottom of highly-polluted and oxygen-deficient water-courses. Rests head downward in the tube with its rear end sticking up and moving rapidly. Twists up into a ball when disturbed. Feeds on mud from the bottom and eats approx. four times its own weight per day. There are sometimes so many together that the muddy bottom looks red. Lays its eggs in cocoons, 0.5 mm long.

egg cocoon x 6

x 6

Stylodrilus heringianus

3-4 cm. White to red with red veins. Two small spines on tenth segment. Found locally, primarily in shallow water and in lakes poor in nutrients, but also found in pure springs and streams.
Swims with spiral movements and curls up like Tubifex if touched.

Lumbriculus variegatus

4-8 cm. Reddish brown with faintly iridescent greenish sheen. Common, found on muddy bottoms, often in fairly deep water among plants in all types of fresh water. Does not construct tubes but anchors itself in the mud with its thick posterior, stiffly or obliquely upright, often together with Tubifex. Swims with spiral movements, and breaks apart easily if handled too roughly.

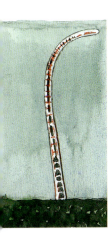

Earthworms

Earthworms are segmented worms with eight small bristles on each segment in paired rows along body.

Square-tailed worm
Eiseniella tetraedra

A very active, aquatic earthworm that can be up to 6 cm long. Often reddish-brown or reddish, but can also be greyish-brown, yellowish-brown, golden or greenish. Forward of saddle, body is cylindrical, to rear it is clearly rectangular in cross section. Very common under stones and moss on the banks of springs and streams, but also lives in ponds and lakes, and can be found completely submerged.

x 1.5

ROUNDWORMS

Roundworms or nematodes are small, 0.1-10 mm long, smooth, non-segmented worms. They are white and glassy. Some of them are parasites. Common in all types of fresh water.

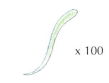

x 100

Mermis sp.

A threadworm. Up to 12 cm. White. The young are parasites in spiders and insects, including grasshoppers, earwigs, caddis flies, black-flies and ants, which often become sterile or die. The adult worms bore their way out and mate, and the female burrows into damp ground, where it can lie dormant for up to two years like a dense tangled cotton thread. In warm, damp weather, after rain or heavy dewfall it emerges, winds around plants and lays its eggs, which are eaten by the hosts.

Gordius aquaticus

A horsehair worm. 12-35 mm long and 0.5-1 mm wide. Male dark brown, female more yellowish; both have a white anterior end ahead of a brownish-black ring. Male has forked posterior end, female has blunt posterior end. Often see many together during mating, in an intertwined bundle. The larva parasitises large diving beetles, particularly of the genus *Dytiscus*. Found locally in springs, streams and rivers.

male's posterior end x 3

Some related species have a complex life cycle, involving parasitising land insects, which are inexplicably drawn to water once the worm is fully developed. *G. albopunctatus*, 16-33 mm, with clear central seam along underside, is also common. Parasitises caddis fly larvae.

Gordius sp. ♀ x 1.5

HYDRAS

Hydras are freshwater coelenterate polyps, resembling miniature sea anemones. They have a sac-shaped body with a mouth surrounded by long tentacles with cnidoblasts that can paralyse prey and hold it. They prey on a wide range of small creatures. Some species live individually, others in colonies. Reproduction takes place by budding throughout the summer and by sexual reproduction in autumn. The dormant eggs overwinter. Hydras contract if touched.

Each cnidoblast has a little sensory hair and contains many nematocysts. Within each nematocyst is a sharp spike, some poison and a long, thin hollow thread. When a small creature touches the sensory hairs, the spikes tear a hole in it, and the threads are flung out and introduce the poison into the wound. In this way the polyp can paralyse water fleas and other small animals, and its tentacles then contract and insert the prey into its mouth.

A small spherical water flea, **Anchistropus emarginatus**, up to 1 mm, is immune to the cnidoblasts' poison. It sticks a pair of spines on the abdominal edge of its shell into the polyp and with powerful spines on its legs tears out pieces of tissue. See illustration p. 130.
The ciliate protistan **Trichodina** can also be found in large numbers on freshwater polyps; it is only visible through a magnifying glass or microscope.

Green Hydra
Hydra viridissima

Body 5-15 mm long, approx. 1 mm wide, narrowest at bottom. Grass-green due to unicellular algae, *Chlorella* sp., that live in the stomach-wall cells. 6-10 tentacles that are slightly shorter than body. Common on plants and stones in ditches, ponds, ornamental pools and lakes. The polyp lives in symbiosis with the algae, i.e. a form of partnership where both parties benefit from the cohabitation: the algae obtain nourishment from the polyp, and in turn supply the polyp with oxygen. It can therefore live in very oxygen-deficient locations. Overwinters as egg.

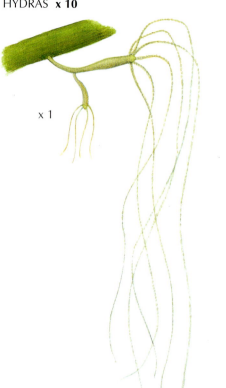

x 1

Hydra oligactis

Body 20-30 mm, stalked. Colour varies greatly. Six tentacles, up to 25 cm long. Very common on plants and stones in lakes and slow-moving water and in late summer can be seen as dense cover on plants. Overwinters both as egg and adult.

Freshwater polyps hold on to their support using a sticky secretion under their basal disc. They can slowly glide along on this, but can also move like inchworms, by bending their body over, holding on with their tentacles and dragging their basal disc forward to a new anchoring point. They can do this about five times per hour and thus move a few cm a day.

Hydra vulgaris

Body approx. 10 mm long and 1 mm wide. Greyish brown and narrowest at bottom. 6-8 tentacles, that can be stretched out to twice or three times the length of the body, and are kept bent downwards at rest. Overwinters as egg. Common on plants and stones in shady places in lakes.

AMOEBAS

Amoebas consist of only a single cell, which reproduces by dividing in two. Most are naked, but some have a protective shell (test). They move using 'false feet', pseudopodia, which are bulges of the cell, and they feed primarily on unicellular algae.

Arcella sp.

A testate (shelled) amoeba. Up to 0.25 mm in diameter. It creates the shell itself from chitin, and it resembles a convex disc. Pale yellow initially, later brown. Common in ponds and lakes on underside of floating leaves and among other aquatic plants. Can be seen with the naked eye as brownish-black pinheads. Many similar species.

Difflugia sp.

A testate amoeba. Up to 0.5 mm in diameter. The shell resembles a jar standing upside down. It is constructed of tiny grains of sand cemented together. Common in ponds and lakes on underside of floating leaves and among other aquatic plants. Many similar species.

HELIOZOANS

Heliozoans (sun animalcules) are unicellular spherical protozoans that may float freely in the water. The skin's radiating extensions, pseudopodia, have an internal rod that disappears when the pseudopodia are drawn in. Reproduction is by simple fission. In some species the individuals stick together, forming colonies.

Actinophrys sol

Approx. 0.05 mm in diameter. Common among plants in ponds and lakes.

x 200

CILIATES

Ciliates have a fixed shape, with a clear mouth, and they reproduce by dividing in two. Their bodies are completely or partially covered by cilia, which both propel the animal forward and fan food towards the mouth. They feed primarily on bacteria and unicellular algae. Some are predators. They are found all year and survive drought and adverse conditions by encasing themselves in a hard shell, a cyst.

Ophrydium versatile

Lives in colonies shaped like a pale-green, glassy and gelatinous lump, which can be up to 10 cm in diameter, resembling an alga, or even part of a higher plant. The colony is made up of many thousands of individuals, in tubes in the gelatinous mass and connected to each other by stalks. Colonies are initially attached to plant stems out to a depth of two metres, but later detach and are found locally floating near banks of lakes.

Colony of *Ophrydium* x 1.5

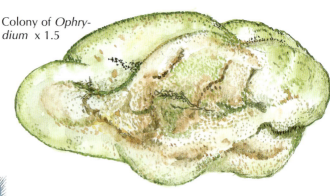

Paramecium caudatum

A slipper animalcule. Up to 0.4 mm. Oblong and slipper-shaped with a mouth in a deep funnel. Feeds primarily on bacteria and unicellular algae. Common in ponds, lakes and slow-moving water.

x 200

Carchesium sp.

A bell animalcule. These bell-shaped creatures, 0.1mm long, rest on long retractile stalks and live in large, branching colonies with several hundred linked animals, attached to plants and animals. When disturbed, the stalk curls up in a spiral. Common in ponds, lakes and slow-moving water.

Vorticella sp.

These bell-shaped creatures rest singly on long stalk muscles in large colonies, like open bells with two ciliar fringes. Reproduction is by longitudinal division. The newly-formed creature is free swimming at first, but later attaches itself to a hard substrate. Colonies can cover plants and animal life in greyish blankets. Common in ponds, lakes and slow-moving water.

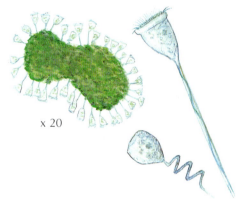

x 20

Stentor sp.

Trumpet-shaped (known as trumpet animalcules), up to 2 mm long, living individually in large colonies. Seen as a bluish-black, green, yellow or brown layer on plants, e.g. under water-lily leaves. The bell can contract if disturbed and change shape. It can also be found free-swimming, egg-shaped and with rounded rear end. Common in ponds, lakes and slow-moving water.

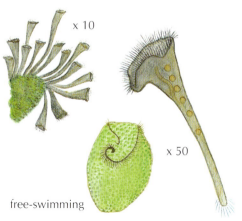

x 10

x 50

free-swimming

ROTIFERS

Rotifers are named after the ring of cilia that form a wheel shape
at the anterior end of the animal (the wheel organ or corona).
Behind this is a broader body, often with a slender foot. The
wheel organ propels the animal forward in the water and
procures food, primarily unicellular plants and animals.
Some are transparent, others have a strong shell around
their body. The foot is slender and ends in two or more toes,
which are used to hold on to its support, or for swimming.
The body often has visible eyespots. The female lays three
types of egg: small male eggs, larger female eggs and
thick-shelled dormant eggs that overwinter. In most rotifers males
are rare and reproduction is normally by parthenogenesis.

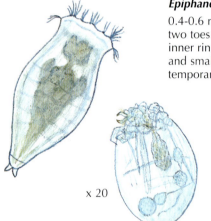

Epiphanes sp.

0.4-0.6 mm. Almost conical with a small foot and
two toes. The outer ciliary ring has long cilia; the
inner ring has bristle-like cilia. Common in puddles
and small ponds with highly-polluted water and small
temporary ponds.

Asplanchna sp.

Up to 1.5 mm. Sac-shaped, unarmoured
and resembles an oblong, crystalline
bubble. No foot. Has two eyespots. Free-
swimming and very common, particularly in spring and autumn in ponds and
lakes. A predator that feeds primarily on
other rotifers, including *Brachionus* and
Keratella.

x 20

Brachionus sp.

0.2-0.3 mm. Elongated and egg-shaped with a red
eye. The skin has thickened into a shell that may
have long spines at front and rear. The foot is usually
annulated with short toes, and can be drawn into the
body. Common free-swimming in larger ponds and
small lakes. Many species.

Some rotifers only develop long spines if living
together with the predators that pursue them.
Thus *Brachionus* has particularly long spines
when living together with *Asplanchna*.

Keratella cochlearis

Approx. 0.2 mm. No foot. Has a strong shell around its body with a red eye and one rear spine. Very common free-swimming in ponds and lakes.
Another species, **K. aculeata**, has two long rear spines. Several species.

Colurella sp.

Common among plants in ponds and lakes.

Monommata sp.

Common among plants in ponds and lakes.

Rotaria sp.

Common among plants in ponds and lakes.

Philodina roseola

0.2-0.5 mm. Red, very elongated and moves like an inchworm on aquatic plants. It can survive very low temperatures and may be present in such large numbers that they turn the water red. Common in ponds and lakes, on damp moss, on trees etc; also in sites subject to drying, e.g bird-baths.

Rotifers are some of the smallest multicellular animals, many of them being smaller than some unicellular creatures. Rotifers also show what is known as cell constancy – all specimens of the same sex within a particular species have the same number of cells in their body.

Conochilus unicornis

Up to 1 mm. Tubular. Often forms circular colonies, linked by tips of feet, with 3-20 animals in each. Common all year in open bodies of water in lakes.
A similar common species, **C. volvo**, lives in colonies of 50-100.

x 50

MOSS ANIMALS

Moss animals are tiny, vase-like creatures with a horseshoe-shaped ring of tentacles. They live in colonies, where individuals are linked to each other. Colonies are present on stones, branches, tree roots, green plants etc. Their shape can vary from long, thin, jointed branches or a thin cover-ing, to small bushes or fleshy lumps that may re-semble sponges. Their food consists of algae, plankton and detritus, which they waft into their mouth with their tentacles. The individual animals reproduce by budding, primarily on the fringes of the colony.

Paludicella articulata

Delicate, branched colonies, straw-coloured to dark reddish brown. Found locally, sometimes as crusty cover on plants, stones etc. in ponds, lakes and slow-moving rivers.

Moss animals survive the winter by producing disc-shaped, brownish overwintering bodies (statoblasts, up to 1.5 mm in diameter), in autumn before the colony dies of cold at the beginning of winter. The statoblasts are surrounded by chitin and drift with waves and currents and form new colonies in spring.

Fredericella sultana

Antler-like colonies, creeping or freely upright, or hanging like vines with weak branches. Dark brown, except the outermost, forked growths. Found in ponds, lakes and slow-moving water, often just under the surface.

Plumatella repens

Colonies begin with small forked branches, but later are dense like a lawn and found as twined lace-like covering on stones, branches etc., or as long thin vines, e.g. under water-lily leaves. Transparent at first, but gradually becoming more or less brown. This genus is common in ponds, lakes and slow-moving rivers.

colony on water-lily x 2

statoblasts

colony x 1

181

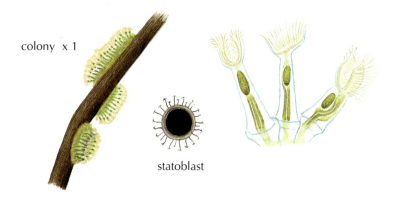

colony x 1

statoblast

Cristatella mucedo

Colonies, up to 30 cm long, large and slimy, resemble an enlarged, hairy caterpillar that is often divided crosswise. They can glide slowly along on thin chitin, which is secreted on the colony's underside. Found locally in ponds, lakes and warm, tranquil river inlets. Seen on aquatic plants, particularly under water-lilies, but also found on tree stumps, roots, stones etc.

Lophopus crystallinus

Colonies grow like a fan or a pouch with several lobes. Soft and gelatinous, up to 4 cm in diameter. Rather local, may be found in ditches, ponds, lakes, streams and rivers, primarily on aquatic plants, tree roots etc.

colony x 1

Moss animals are also called bryozoans.

FRESHWATER SPONGES

Sponges are colonies of multicellular animals. They appear as green, yellowish or grey, porous finger-shaped branching formations or gelatinous lumps on posts, roots, pieces of wood and stones in ponds, lakes and watercourses. A sponge can be 30 cm in diameter, but is seldom more than a few cm across. They are immobile and firmly fixed to the substratum. The individual animals in the sponge feed by filtering small particles from the water, which they can guide in through the small ducts to chambers within the sponge and out of the large apertures using their cilia. The sponge's skeleton consists of small siliceous needles, spicules.

Ephydatia fluviatilis

Has flat lobes and smooth siliceous needles. Very common, particularly on stones in moderately fast-flowing water (not illustrated).

Ephydatia is often attacked by caddis fly larvae, of the genus *Ceraclea* (see p. 23).

A sponge produces eggs and sperm cells. Fertilisation occurs in the ducts, and tiny, rounded, ciliated larvae swim out to settle elsewhere and form a new sponge

overwintering body (gemmule)   x 15

x 6

Freshwater sponges overwinter as small, 1 mm brownish bodies, known as gemmules, consisting of a small group of cells surrounded by spicules and coated with a chitin-like substance. These sprout into new sponges in spring.

Spongilla lacustris

Branched, except in fast-flowing water, and has spiny siliceous needles. Very common.

2 forms of *Spongilla lacustris*

FRESHWATER FISH

Roach
Rutilus rutilus

Rarely over 200 g. Normally 10-25 cm. Slender,
shiny and silvery. Eyes and pelvic and anal fins reddish, pectoral fins more yellow. Pelvic fins attached
just below front edge of dorsal fin. Spawns April-June
in fairly shallow water, often on stony bottoms, sometimes among aquatic plants. The eggs stick firmly to
plants and stones. The young fish live in shoals and
initially eat planktonic animals, later larger invertebrates, algae and soft leaves of aquatic plants. Grows
to 6-7 cm in first year. Very common in shallow
water among plants in ponds, lakes and slow-moving
water, but can swim upstream in streams and rivers
with fairly strong currents. Also found in brackish
water.

Bleak
Alburnus alburnus

Rarely over 40 g. Normally 15-20 cm. Slender and
silvery, with upward-pointing mouth. Grey fins.
Spawns in fairly shallow water with a hard bottom,
May-July. The eggs stick firmly to stones and
branches.
Fry feed on planktonic animals, the young fish on
small invertebrates. Grows to 3-5 cm in first year.
Shoaling fish found primarily in the outermost broad
belt in clear-water lakes and slow-moving water.
Often snaps up flying insects,
jumping out of
the water.

tufted loosestrife

Crucian Carp
Carassius carassius

Rarely over 1 kg. Normally 15-25 cm. Plump, high-backed and yellowish brown with dark fins and long dorsal fin. Spawns May-June among plants. Lacks the barbels of the true carp. Fry feed on planktonic animals; the young fish on invertebrates and soft plant matter, and can be found in small shoals in shallow water. Can tolerate both lack of oxygen and winter cold and thrives in marshy, very murky waters where no other fish can survive, e.g. in village ponds. Under favourable conditions grows to 6 cm after one year. Prefers shallow boggy ponds and small lakes.

Pike *Esox lucius*

Female largest, but rarely over 10 kg. Male rarely over 3 kg. Normally 50-100 cm. Broad, flat snout. Mouth has many powerful, pointed teeth. Elongated body, upper and underside almost parallel. Dorsal and anal fin identical and positioned well back on body. A predatory fish that hunts best by sight; lurking still, then rushing forward to surprise its prey. Spawns March-May in very shallow water, when the dorsal fins can sometimes be seen from a distance. The eggs stick firmly to plants, and the newly-hatched larvae remain there passively until umbilical sac has been eaten up. Larva feeds initially on planktonic animals, the young fish on small animals and other fish. It keeps to shallow water and grows to 15-20 cm in first year. Thrives best in clear water. Common in ponds, lakes and slow-moving rivers. Also found in brackish water and can tolerate fairly acidic water too.

larva x 3

adult x 1/5

water dock

Perch
Perca fluviatilis

Rarely over 1 kg. Normally 25-40 cm. Deep body, greenish yellow with broad dark transverse stripes. Red pelvic, anal and caudal fins. Front dorsal fin has spiny rays and a black spot at rear. Powerful spine on gill covers. A predatory fish that lives in shoals. However, the largest ones live alone. Spawns in April in shallow water with vegetation. Lays its eggs in 1-2 m long continuous strings like paper chains on plants and stones. The larvae live initially in the upper water layers. The young fish favour shallow water among plants and feed initially on planktonic animals, and subsequently primarily on small bottom-dwelling animals. Grows to 3-5 cm in first year. Thrives best in clear water. Common in ponds, lakes and slow-moving water. Also found in brackish water and can also tolerate fairly acidic water.

Many fish have sticky eggs that are laid in shallow water. These can stick to feathers and legs of ducks and other aquatic birds, and in this way are spread from water to water. Newly-dug ponds can therefore gain a fish population surprisingly quickly.

Perch eggs

Ten-spined Stickleback
Pungitius pungitius

4-7 cm. 8-11 free spiny rays on its back. Male builds nest, like three-spined stickleback. Common in all types of fresh water, but primarily in murky waterholes and ditches and in shallow inlets in brackish water.

Sticklebacks are an important link in the freshwater food chain. They eat a mass of small creatures and are in turn eaten by various types of edible fish, such as pike, perch, trout and eels.

Three-spined Stickleback
Gasterosteus aculeatus

5-11 cm. 3 free spiny rays on its back and bony plates on each side. Male has red underparts in spawning season. Builds a nest of plant matter, which he defends from others, and into which the female is lured. Some live in shoals in salt water near the coast, but migrate to rivers and lakes to spawn, March-July. Others live in murky ponds, ditches or streams.

broad-leaved
pondweed

♂ in spawning season

AMPHIBIANS

Amphibians, like fish, are cold-blooded vertebrates. There are two groups represented in Europe – the frogs and toads which lack tails as adults, and the newts and salamanders which have tails both as adults and larvae. Mating takes place in water. The eggs have no outer shell and develop into larvae (tadpoles) that live in water and breathe via gills. Newt tadpoles have three feathery outer gills. The gills of frog and toad tadpoles are quickly covered by a fold of skin. Tadpoles metamorphose gradually and ultimately breathe via lungs. In frogs and toads the hind legs develop first; in newts the forelegs develop first. With frogs and toads, females are usually larger than males; vice versa with newts.

tadpoles
in 4 stages

inside of inner toe of hind leg showing tubercle

Frog and toad tadpoles filter small organic particles from the water, which they eat. They also rasp algae and other material from the bottom, off aquatic plants, stones etc. with their tiny teeth.

Common Frog *Rana temporaria*

50-111 mm, but rarely over 90 mm. Female larger. Snout usually fairly blunt. Colour varies greatly. Generally brown, light brown or olive-green with dark spots, but can be yellowish, reddish, grey or almost completely black. Underside is usually completely white, but can be spotted, particularly in centre, and often has a yellow colouring in the groin area. In the breeding season males may have a bluish sheen. Tubercle is shorter than innermost joint of inner toe. Normally breeds mid-April. Young males overwinter in water. Very common.

Lays its eggs in clumps of 1,500-3,000, often in very shallow water, less than 20 cm deep. They rest on the bottom initially, but later rise up to the surface. The tadpole, up to 45 mm, has an oval body. Its tail is 1.5-2 times as long as its body, usually with a blunt tip. Has 3-4 rows of teeth at top of mouth and 4 at bottom.

Moor Frog
Rana arvalis

35-75 mm. Male has more powerful forelegs than female. Resembles common frog, but often has a more pointed snout, is thinner and has longer legs. Tubercle is longer than innermost joint of inner toe, and is higher and harder to the touch than in common frog. Ground colour light brown or brownish orange, with a black spot on temple, a V-shaped patch on neck and dark spots on back. Also has a yellow stripe down centre of back and a thinner yellow stripe down across back from each eye. Found in several colour variations. Some lack the yellow central stripe. Male can be light blue or bluish violet in the breeding season, which is normally mid-April. Usually overwinters in water. This species is found in central Europe, north to Scandinavia and east to the Netherlands.

Lays its eggs (spawn) in clumps with 1,000-2,000 in each, usually at a depth of 10-25 cm, and they do not rise to the surface as quickly as those of common frogs.

The tadpole, up to 48 mm long, is lighter coloured than the common frog's, slightly shorter and fatter, and its tail is evenly pointed. 2-3 rows of teeth at top of the mouth and 3 rows at bottom.

tadpole and adult frog

inside of inner toe of hind leg showing tubercle

below: frogspawn

Frogs lay their eggs in clumps. Toads lay their eggs in long strings. The central nucleus of each egg is surrounded by a blob of protective transparent jelly that also acts like a mini greenhouse.

The egg is warmed by the sun during the day, and the gelatinous mass insulates it and ensures that the warmth does not easily escape. The nuclei of frog and toad eggs are circular, and the embryos have a concave back.

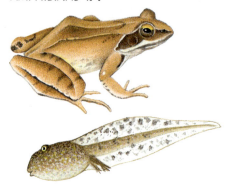

Lays its eggs in clumps with approx. 1,000 in each at a depth of 10-40 cm, but sometimes in fairly deep water. They rise up to the surface after a few weeks.

The tadpole, up to 65 mm, has a long tail, 2-2.5 times longer than its body, and pale, fairly short gills. Its back is light brown or reddish brown with dark spots. Its belly is white with yellow speckles. The tail fringes have large and small black spots.

Agile Frog *Rana dalmatina*

Female 50-70 mm, male 42-60 mm. Resembles Common and Moor Frog, but is thinner and has very long hind legs. Can hop very long distances. Back can have a few dark spots. Has powerful, red toe-joint nodes on underside of hind feet. Males can be blackish brown in the breeding season, March-April, 10-20 days before the common frog breeds. Often found further from the water than other brown frogs, generally in deciduous woodland. Overwinters buried in soil. This species is mainly found in central and southern Europe, with some colonies as far north as Denmark and Sweden.

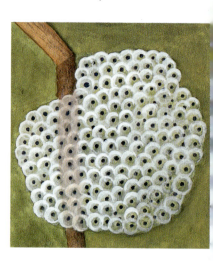

Marsh Frog *Rana ridibunda*

Female 65-130 mm, male 52-105 mm. Resembles Edible Frog, but its colouring is generally more muddy and brownish. Greenish back stripe. Usually found among plants in water. The largest native European frog. Breeds earlier then the Edible Frog, May-June. Its croak can resemble gruff intermittent laughter. Overwinters in water. Lives in larger pools than the Edible Frog. Introduced to certain sites in Brit-

ain – notably Romney Marsh in Kent. Lays its eggs in clumps of 200-2,000 on aquatic plants just under the surface of the water. All eggs in the clump are almost the same size.

The tadpole, up to 85 mm, has a greyish-green back with black and white spots, greyish-white belly, and its throat is generally completely white. Its tail is long and pointed, 1.9-2.3 times longer than its body.

Edible Frog
Rana esculenta

Female 60-110 mm, male 55-96 mm. Large and powerful, green with dark spots and light back stripe. Dark transverse stripes on hind legs. Belly white with black spots. Likes the sun and often sits sunbathing on the bank, but will jump into the water if approached. Lays its eggs late and requires warm water. Breeds late May to June, and croaks day and night throughout early summer. The young frogs almost always overwinter on land. The adults overwinter either in water or buried on land, often in water holes near woodland. Also thrives in brackish water. Widespread in Europe. Known from a few sites in southern England (introduced). This frog originated as a hybrid between the Marsh Frog *(R. ridibunda)* and the Pool Frog *(R. lessonae)*. The latter has recently been shown to be possibly native in Britain; it is found in a few sites in the south.

Egg nuclei can vary greatly in size. Lays its eggs in clumps of 200-300 on

aquatic plants, approx. 10 cm under the surface of the water. If a clump is picked up, it will often break apart. The tadpole's back is olive-green or olive-brown and densely spotted, and it has a light area around the eyes. Pale yellow belly with shiny pink or bronze areas. The tail fringes have olive-brown spots. Its tail is 1.5-2 times longer than its body. Normally up to 60-80 mm, but can grow longer than 100 mm.

Adult edible frogs are fierce predators. They will eat anything that moves and that they can catch and swallow, e.g. hornets, bumblebees and even young birds. They also eat other frogs, including smaller edible frogs.

Tadpole and egg mass

Common Spadefoot *Pelobates fuscus*

39-80 mm. Females larger than males. Pale greyish-green upperside with large chestnut-brown spots. Belly white with brown dots. Stocky with short legs, and resembles a small toad. No visible ear drum and no webbing on forefeet. Large protruding eyes with vertical pupil. May release garlic smell if disturbed. Breeds April-May in sunny water holes without fish. Outside the breeding season it stays on land, buried during the day and only emerging in total darkness. Also overwinters buried on land. Found locally, mainly in central and eastern Europe, west to northern France.

Lays its eggs in 5-8 longitudinal rows in a 15-80 cm-long egg 'sausage', 15-20 mm in diameter, twisted around aquatic plants.
The tadpole, up to 13 mm, is initially dull greyish green to yellowish brown, later ochre-coloured to olive-brown. Its tail fin extends forward to the middle of the back.

Tree Frog *Hyla arborea*

33-50 mm. Small and stocky with thin legs. Shiny, plain green on upperside, lighter on belly. However, colouring can change and be brown. At low temperatures it can be greenish black and at high temperatures yellow. It has adhesive disks at the ends of its toes and climbs and jumps around in bushes, undergrowth and tall grass, seldom coming down to the ground. It requires warm, pure water with no fish and breeds May-June. Overwinters in holes in the ground, cavities in trees and in stone walls and masonry. Can endure being completely frozen. Has been introduced to Britain and may persist in a site in the New Forest.
Lays its eggs in walnut-size clumps of up to 130 eggs, attached to aquatic plants just under the surface of the water. If a clump is picked up, it will often break apart.
The tadpole, up to 50 mm, has a brownish or olive-coloured back with golden dots. Its belly is shiny golden or copper-coloured. The tail fringes are yellowish, plain or have dark spots.

Fire-bellied Toad *Bombina bombina*

37-56 mm. Small and toad-like. Protruding eyes with triangular pupils.
Upperside greyish brown, dark brown
or almost black with numerous warts
and greyish-black spots. Underside
black or bluish-black with large orange-
red spots and small white dots. Breeds
best in sunny shallow small ponds with
no fish, May-June. Its croaking can be
heard from a great distance and can
resemble a cuckoo's call, or the sound
from blowing air across the top of an
empty bottle. Overwinters on land in
mouseholes, stone walls, under tree
roots etc. This is mainly an eastern
European species, with a range extending west to Denmark and south to
Slovenia and northern Croatia.

Lays its eggs in loose clumps with up to
130 in each, often deposited like paper
chains around plant stems and on the
bottom.

The tadpole, up to 37-59 mm, has an
almost spherical body, and tail fringes
with a distinct reticular design of criss-
crossing black lines. Large, triangular
mouth with three double rows of lower
teeth and two rows of upper teeth.

The Fire-bellied Toad is poisonous
and not eaten by many animals.
The black and orange pattern on its
underside functions as warning colours, as do the yellow and black
stripes of a wasp and a ladybird's
red colouring. If a fire-bellied toad
feels threatened and cannot escape,
it will turn on its back and perhaps
in this way avoid being attacked.

Each year amphibians will often
visit the water where they lived as
a tadpole. However, new, suitable
water holes will quickly become
populated.

Frogs and toads have very strong breeding instincts.
The male clings to the female with his forelegs to
wait for (and perhaps stimulate), her to spawn the
eggs, so he can fertilise them externally with his
sperm. Several males may cling to one female, and
the fight over her can be so fierce that she may
drown under the weight of the competing males.

egg string of Common Toad

Common Toad
Bufo bufo

Female 77-120 mm, male 53-78 mm. Back light brown or greyish with small or large dark-brown spots; belly whitish with small dark spots. Dry, warty skin. Fairly short hind legs. Red eyes with horizontal pupils, and behind each eye is an oblong poison gland. It crawls more than it hops, and males may make a noise if prodded. Breeds March-April, also in brackish water. Lives on land outside the breeding season; females slightly further from the water than males. Overwinters buried in the ground. Common throughout most of Europe, but absent from Ireland and Mediterranean islands.

Lays its eggs in strings, which wind around aquatic plants, twigs or branches. Each string is 5-8 mm thick, in 3-4 rows if not stretched out, otherwise in two rows. The tadpoles are flattened, initially completely black, later slightly lighter on belly, with yellow dots. Small rectangular mouth. Row of teeth at top of mouth with a gap in centre. The tadpoles are often seen swimming in dense shoals.

The Common Toad large tadpoles are poisonous to fish. The adult toads are also poisonous to most animals. However, hedgehogs can tolerate the poison, and rub their quills in the poisonous secretion from the toad's skin to protect themselves. Badgers and buzzards avoid the poison by biting a hole in the belly and only eating the insides. The greenbottle fly **Lucilia bufonivora**, lays its eggs on the back of a toad. The larvae crawl into the toad through the eye hollows and nostrils and feed on its brain, and on the rest of its body when the toad dies after a few days. The larvae then pupate in the toad's dead body.

common toad: tadpoles and adult

Natterjack (toad)
Bufo calamita

43-80 mm. Small and stocky with fairly short hind legs, and almost no webbing. Brownish, but can be lighter or darker, with a number of darker, often greenish, spots, and usually with a yellow back stripe. Yellowish-green eyes with horizontal pupils. Very rarely hops, but runs like a mouse. Breeds primarily in pools, preferably with bare edges, in dune-slacks, gravel pits, lowland heaths etc., May-June. Can stand brackish water and therefore also breeds in pools in salt meadows etc. Only active at night, and hides during the day in holes in the ground on land. Thrives best on bare ground, gravel or sand. Overwinters buried on land. Found mainly in western Europe, from Iberia to Britain, Ireland and Scandinavia.

Lays its eggs in 1-2 m long double strings. Each string is approx. 2-6 mm thick. The tadpoles are flattened, almost completely black with dark-grey belly. Smaller mouth than Common Toad, and often has a light-grey spot on throat. Tadpoles grow to only 22-30 mm long.

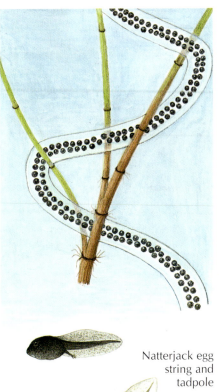

Natterjack egg string and tadpole

Green Toad tadpole

Green Toad *Bufo viridis*

50-100 mm, but rarely over 85 mm. Female larger than male. Warty back, light grey with large green spots and smaller red spots, but turns dark in cold. Breeds from late April to June, preferably in sunny and almost completely bare water holes with no fish or other amphibians; also in brackish water. Overwinters in holes in the ground. Male croaks with high ringing tones that merge into a prolonged flutelike note. Mainly central and eastern Europe.

Lays its eggs in 2-5 m long double strings around submerged grasses or on the bottom. Each string is 4-8 mm thick. The tadpole, up to 53 mm, is not quite as flat as with the other toads. It is initially completely black with yellow dots on belly, later has light belly, dark-grey, light-grey or brownish back with numerous light spots, or mottled with black and bronze spots.

Smooth Newt *Triturus vulgaris*

6-10 cm. Outside the mating season has a soft, velvety skin and a fairly low fringe along its back. Brown back with greyish-black spots. Dark longitudinal stripes on head. Belly orange in centre and whitish at sides, with large, round, dark-grey spots in male. Female's belly is at most only dotted. In the mating season the female has a low fringe over her back; male an unbroken high dorsal crest and a light-blue stripe on underside of tail. Breeds primarily in very small, partially shaded still water, preferably with no fish, April-May.

Outside the breeding season it lives on land near the water, emerging at night and hiding under stones, logs etc. during the day. Feeds on small animals. Overwinters on land. Common in most of Europe, except the south.

Lays its eggs individually on leaves of aquatic plants. The tadpole, up to 40 mm, is yellowish-brown to orange-brown on upperside. Underside is pale yellow. Its gills are brownish red and feathery.

eggs x 2

x 2

newly-hatched
and older
tadpole

Palmate Newt *Triturus helveticus*

This is the smallest newt in north-west Europe. It resembles the Smooth Newt, but the breeding male has webbed hind feet and a filament at the tip of its tail.

♂

♀

♀

(Great) Crested Newt
Triturus cristatus

Known also as Warty Newt. 10-16 cm. Many warts on skin, which may be white at sides. Back dark grey or blackish brown with black spots. Throat is dark and muddy-coloured and belly bright yellow or orange with large black spots. Female has yellow cloaca, male's is black. In the mating season the female has swimming fringe on upper and underside of tail. Yellow on underside. Male has a high, wavy or serrated dorsal crest that ends just before the base of tail. The tail fringe is also slightly wavy, serrated, and in centre of tail on each side a white translucent band develops. Breeds primarily in small, sunny waters, preferably with no fish, April-July.

The adults live on land July-September. A predator that feeds mainly on earthworms, snails, millipedes and other, slightly larger invertebrates.
Overwinters on land. Most of Europe except the south. Local in Britain but absent from Ireland.
The eggs are pale greenish-yellow and slightly larger than those of Smooth Newt.
The tadpole, up to 80 mm, is greyish-black on back with black spots, light grey on sides and white on belly. Often swims freely in the water and is more exposed to predators than Smooth Newt larvae.
In Britain this species has declined due to habitat destruction and is strictly protected.

Tadpole

♂

When amphibians hibernate on land, they absorb the necessary oxygen through their skin. Adult newts shed their skin frequently; it is stripped off like a stocking and eaten.

Newts lay eggs individually on leaves, that are then folded up over the eggs. The egg nuclei are oval, and the embryo has a convex back.

Newt larvae are initially pale yellowish-brown with dark longitudinal stripes, the species almost indistinguishable from one another while small. The tadpoles are predators that feed on various aquatic animals. After metamorphosis they go on to land and do not come back to the water until their second year, once they are sexually mature.

Alpine Newt
Triturus alpestris

7-12 cm. Female has ochre-coloured or orange belly; underside of tail more yellowish. Side has a band of black spots and white warts. Back is marbled greyish-blue or greyish-brown and lacks dorsal crest. Male has orange-red belly, light sides with large, round dark spots and a narrow pale blue band. Back plain bluish-grey to blue with a fairly low pale-yellow dorsal crest with black spots. Breeds April-July in small ponds, usually shady, and may also be found in larger lakes. Lives on land outside the breeding season, primarily in deciduous woodland. Found from northern Spain to Denmark. In Britain introduced to a few sites in the south. Overwinters on land.

The tadpole is initially pale yellowish-brown with dark longitudinal stripes, like all other newt larvae. It gains large brown gills and gradually takes on adult colouration; up to 50 mm long.

REPTILES

Reptiles are cold-blooded vertebrates, just like amphibians, that can only partially regulate their own body temperature. They have skin with scales or horn plates that protect their body. Most lay their eggs in a rather soft, parchment-like shell, some in a harder calcareous shell. The entire embryonic development takes place in the egg. Reptiles include snakes, lizards, crocodiles and tortoises and turtles.

Grass Snake
Natrix natrix

Female up to 130 cm, male up to 50-90 cm. Although the female is larger, the male has a relatively longer tail. Lacks the zigzag stripes of Adder. Generally black or dark grey with two yellow spots on back of head, but the spots may be indistinct. Lives mainly near water and in marshes. Active April-October. The mating season is April-May.

In June-July the female lays 10-30 eggs in a warm place, a compost heap, a pile of rotting leaves, rush debris, rotting straw etc. The eggs hatch in September, and the young that emerge are 15-20 cm long. They become sexually mature at approx. 4 years old. Feeds almost exclusively on amphibians and fish.

Grass Snakes are inoffensive animals that do no harm to humans. If it feels threatened, a Grass Snake may lie on its back and play dead, with an open mouth. It rarely bites and is not venomous. If picked up, it may discharge a yellowish, viscous fluid from its anal glands. This has a penetrating rank odour and is difficult to wash off clothes. Unlike the Adders, the Grass Snake has such strong muscles that it can twist up around someone's arm if being held by its tail.

The skin of a snake is not slimy, as is often stated; it is covered with dry, overlapping scales.

Animals on floating leaves

The floating leaves of water-lilies and pondweeds have their own unique fauna, found nowhere else. Young leaves are often unaffected, but once they have been on the surface of the water some time, you can see animals or traces of them on the leaves. Many animals use them to lay eggs on, and the larvae of some small animals feed on them. By autumn they are often completely ragged and eaten through.

Galerucella nymphaea
(see p. 113)

Numerous other animals use water-lily leaves as a resting-place, e.g. beetles, pond skaters, dragonflies and damselflies. They are also used by a number of small animals to lay their eggs on.

Paraponyx stratiota (see p. 10)
The larva mines the leaf.

Nymphula stagnata (see p. 8)
The larva mines the leaf.

Mesovelia furcata (see p. 96)

Hydromyza livens (see p. 72)
The larva mines the leaf.

Nymphula nymphaeata
(see p. 9)
The larva feeds on the
leaf.

Arcella sp.
(see p. 175)

Difflugia sp.
(see p. 175)

Stentor sp.
(see p. 177)

Ripistes parasita
(see p. 169)

Nymphula stagnata (see p. 8)
The larva pupates using a
piece of leaf as a cover.

Animals on the lower surface of water-lilies

Plumatella repens
(see p. 181)

Cristatella mucedo
(see p. 182)

Lophopus crystallinus
(see p. 182)

On the underside of water-lily leaves you may also find many coelenterates, amoebas, ciliates, moss animals, freshwater sponges etc. Snails also browse on the many microscopic creatures found here.

The surface film

The upper layer of the water surface is called the surface film. Many small animals find it difficult to break through, and the surface tension is capable of supporting a pin or a light coin. It is therefore also capable of supporting insects and other small animals. The load-bearing capability of the surface film is greatest in ponds and lakes with still water.

Dolichopus ungulatus (see p. 73)

Hebrus pusillus, a small bug (see p. 96)

Adult and nymph of **Gerris lacustris**, a pond skater (see p. 97)

Podura aquatica, a springtail (see p. 118)

Animals on the surface film

Many small animals make use of the support provided by the surface film by running about on it. A lot of small animals lay eggs that drift along on the surface film. Other animals change from pupa to adult while clinging to the surface of the water. You can often find the empty pupal cases blown together along the bank.

Gyrinus **sp.,** a whirligig beetle
(see p. 98)

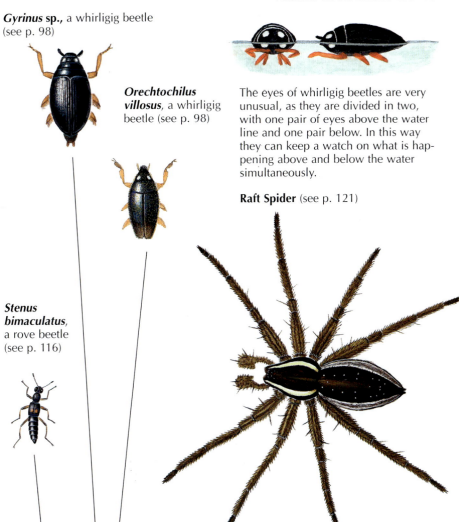

Orechtochilus villosus, a whirligig beetle (see p. 98)

The eyes of whirligig beetles are very unusual, as they are divided in two, with one pair of eyes above the water line and one pair below. In this way they can keep a watch on what is happening above and below the water simultaneously.

Raft Spider (see p. 121)

Stenus bimaculatus, a rove beetle (see p. 116)

Animals on the underside of the surface film

Many small animals make use of the surface film by hanging beneath it. Some small animals, however, only hang from the film when renewing their air supply, e.g. backswimmers and water boatmen, scavenger beetles, diving beetles etc. Other insects hang from the surface film as pupae and change from pupa to adult while clinging to the surface of the water.

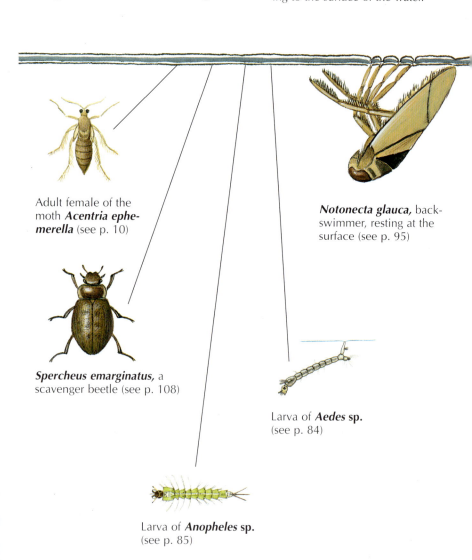

Adult female of the moth *Acentria ephemerella* (see p. 10)

Notonecta glauca, backswimmer, resting at the surface (see p. 95)

Spercheus emarginatus, a scavenger beetle (see p. 108)

Larva of *Aedes* **sp.** (see p. 84)

Larva of *Anopheles* **sp.** (see p. 85)

The surface film is so strong that many food particles remain suspended from it. This is exploited by some animals, including the **Great Pond Snail** (see p. 149) and the ramshorn snail, **_Planorbis vortex_** (see p. 152), which crawl along on the underside of the film. You can clearly see the muscle movements of the snails' feet as they slowly move along.

However, a snail hanging from the surface film is very vulnerable to predators. They will therefore immediately drop down to the bottom if you touch their antennae or create a shadow with your hand.

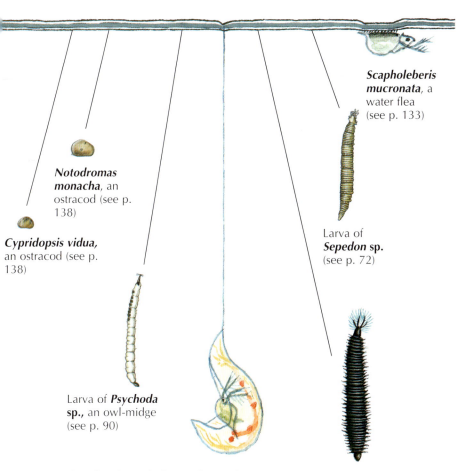

Scapholeberis mucronata, a water flea (see p. 133)

Notodromas monacha, an ostracod (see p. 138)

Cypridopsis vidua, an ostracod (see p. 138)

Larva of **_Sepedon_ sp.** (see p. 72)

Larva of **_Psychoda_ sp.**, an owl-midge (see p. 90)

Mesostoma ehrenbergi, a turbellarian, hangs down from the surface of the water by a mucus thread and makes a kind of basket trap (see p. 158)

Larva of **_Pericoma_ sp.**, an owl-midge (see p. 90)

Pools and temporary ponds

Temporary ponds tend to form in spring and dry up in summer. However, some may re-form after autumn rainfall. These special habitats contain rather unusual species which cannot survive elsewhere. Some insect species only use such ponds as intermediate stations and fly away when they dry up. The volume of water is usually rather small, and the water temperature fluctuates greatly according to the season, and also to some extent reflects daily temperatures. In winter such sites often freeze.

Larva of **Mochlonyx culici-formis,** a phantom midge (see p. 82)

Dalyella viridis, a turbellarian (see p. 158)

Animals in temporary pools

A common characteristic of animals in temporary pools is that they can either endure desiccation in some way, or are capable of flying to another body of water when the pool dries up. This animal community has relatively few species, and the animals are very specialised.

Some small animals are able to live in such habitats, even though you can also find them in other places, e.g. in ditches, small ponds etc.

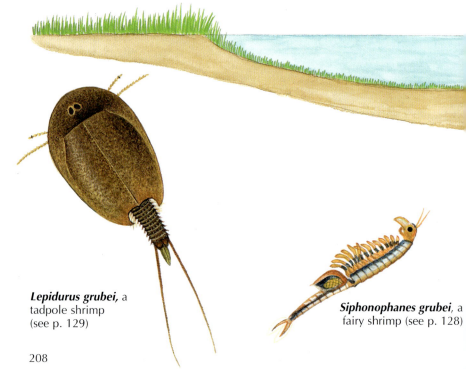

Lepidurus grubei, a tadpole shrimp (see p. 129)

Siphonophanes grubei, a fairy shrimp (see p. 128)

Egg-raft, larva and pupa of
Culex pipiens (see p. 86)

Larva of ***Anopheles* sp.** (see p. 85)

Larva of ***Aedes* sp.** (see p. 84)

Larva of pond olive
Cloeon dipterum, a mayfly
(see p. 55)

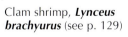

Clam shrimp, ***Lynceus brachyurus*** (see p. 129)

Smooth Newt (see p. 196)

Algal plankton

Lakes and ponds contain a myriad of microscopic phytoplankton, that float freely in the water. This is made up almost exclusively of uni-cellular algae, which can sometimes form colonies, 0.01-0.1 mm in size, occasionally up to 1 mm.

They form the first link in the food chain, as they can utilise solar energy directly. Algal plankton is therefore extremely important for animal life in standing water. If it were not there, the animal life in the water would be much less diverse.

Plankton algae may be divided into different groups according to attri-butes such as shape and colour, and include diatoms, blue-green algae, green algae, golden-brown algae, dinoflagellates etc.

In particularly warm years, there can be mass occurrences of some algae if there are sufficient nutrients for them. Such mass occurrences (algal blooms) can make lake waters completely turbid and result in the formation of poisonous substances that can be dangerous to animals and humans.

Star-shaped diatom

Zig-zag diatom

Above: 2 examples of **diatoms**. These tend to be most abundant in spring.

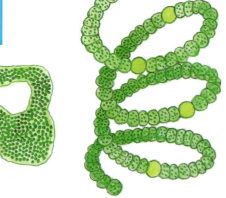

A filamentous blue-green alga

Microcystis sp.

Anabaena sp.

Above: 3 examples of **blue-green algae**. These are organisms without nuclei, closely related to bacteria; often classified as cyanobacteria.

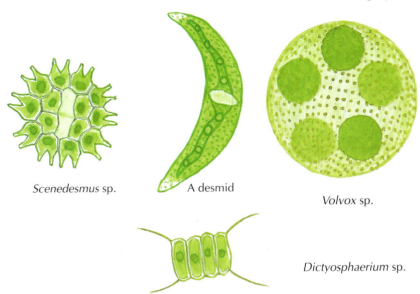

Scenedesmus sp.

A desmid

Volvox sp.

Dictyosphaerium sp.

Above: 4 examples of **green algae,** a very large and diverse group.

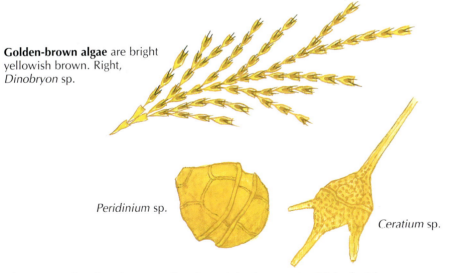

Golden-brown algae are bright yellowish brown. Right, *Dinobryon* sp.

Peridinium sp.

Ceratium sp.

Above: *Dinoflagellates* have two flagella and tiny brown or reddish plastids.

211

The food chain in a clean lake

In a lake, the food chain begins with the phyto-plankton, which consists mostly of small unicellular algae. These are eaten (in this example) by zooplankton, e.g. water fleas, which are eaten by phantom midge larvae and roach, which in turn are eaten by perch or pike, which may then be eaten by cormorants, herons, osprey or otter. Dead planktonic organisms etc. sink to the bottom of the lake and are eaten by worms, non-biting midge larvae and bivalves.

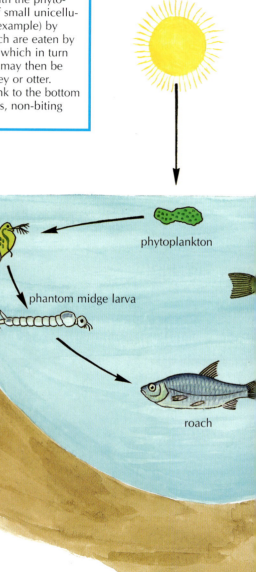

phytoplankton

water flea

phantom midge larva

roach

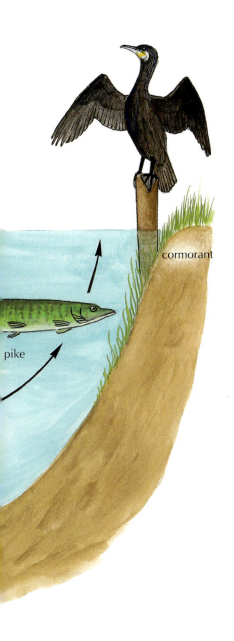

cormorant

pike

Nutrient pollution

The nutrient content of many lakes and rivers is too high, and has increased in the last 50 years. This is due to discharge of waste water, seepage and leaching of nutrients from agriculture, and air pollution. Nutrients from fish farming have also polluted a number of lakes and watercourses. This process of over-enrichment with nutrients is known as eutrophication.

If the supply of nutrients increases, the volume of plankton rises tremendously, and the water becomes opaque. This means that predatory fish like pike can no longer hunt effectively, so there will be more and more roach, which eat the zooplankton, resulting in even more algae. This overproduction of algae results in a larger quantity of dead algae falling to the bottom, where there are insufficient animals to eat them. They will therefore decompose, consuming the oxygen. This means that only a few species can live here, e.g. red non-biting midge larvae.

If there is a total lack of oxygen, a bottom upheaval may occur, where the poisonous gases that have developed in the mud are released, killing many living organisms. This vicious circle can be broken by cutting off the supply of nutrients and removing large quantities of the zooplankton-eating fish.

Lakes are more vulnerable than rivers and streams to nutrient pollution. This is due to the fact that the renewal of water takes place very slowly. It can take several years for the water in a large lake to be replaced.

Swarming

Primarily on calm evenings, or after gentle summer rain, you may see large numbers of insects swarming at the water's edge or above the open water. It is usually the males that fly, perhaps to display themselves or to show the females where they are. When they are ready the females will fly into the swarm to find a mate. Swarms normally develop on the lee side of trees, but in calm weather they are mostly above the tree tops. There can be so many animals in a swarm that from a distance it resembles smoke from a fire.

Swarming insects:

China-mark moths (p. 8-10)
Caddis flies (p. 11-33)
Spongefly (p. 35)
Mayflies (p. 52-59)
Dance-flies (p. 73)
Crane-flies (p. 74-75)
Non-biting midges (p. 78-80)
Procladius **sp.** (p. 81)
Phantom midges (p. 82)
Midges (p. 87)

swarming mayflies

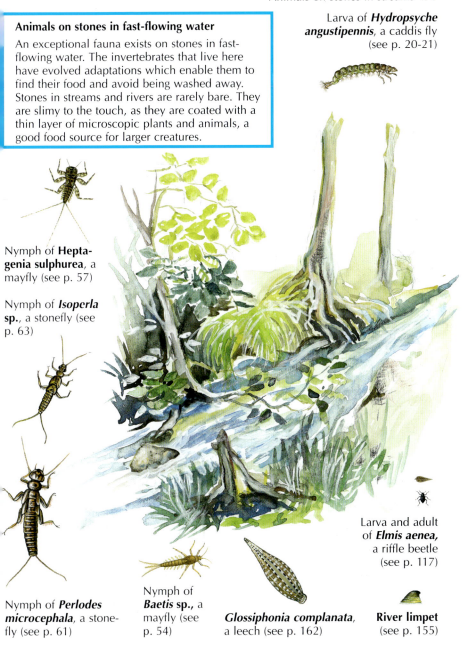

Animals on stones in fast-flowing water

An exceptional fauna exists on stones in fast-flowing water. The invertebrates that live here have evolved adaptations which enable them to find their food and avoid being washed away. Stones in streams and rivers are rarely bare. They are slimy to the touch, as they are coated with a thin layer of microscopic plants and animals, a good food source for larger creatures.

Larva of **Hydropsyche angustipennis**, a caddis fly (see p. 20-21)

Nymph of **Heptagenia sulphurea**, a mayfly (see p. 57)

Nymph of **Isoperla sp.**, a stonefly (see p. 63)

Larva and adult of **Elmis aenea,** a riffle beetle (see p. 117)

Nymph of **Perlodes microcephala**, a stonefly (see p. 61)

Nymph of **Baetis sp.**, a mayfly (see p. 54)

Glossiphonia complanata, a leech (see p. 162)

River limpet (see p. 155)

Aquatic habitats have self-purifying qualities

Pollution by waste water from a sewer produces a characteristic chain of events in a river or other body of water. Close to the discharge there is almost no dissolved oxygen, and only rat-tailed maggots and other animals that can breathe from the surface via a breathing tube can survive there. Downstream is a zone where – at times at least – there is slightly more oxygen. There may be large bacterial plumes here, and on the bottom large numbers of Tubifex worms, which can survive in oxygen-deficient water thanks to the haemoglobin in their blood.

Further downstream more and more species begin to appear, until the water is pure again. How far the polluted zone stretches naturally depends on the volume of waste water, but to an equal extent on the physical characteristics of the watercourse. In a natural watercourse with a swift current the pollutants will very quickly be recycled, whereas the same volume of waste water in a slow-moving canal will result in much longer-lasting pollution. The difference lies in the watercourse's 'self-purifying abilities'.

Larva of *Psychoda* sp., an owl-midge (see p. 90)

Bacterial plume (see p.217)

Water slater (see p. 127)

Larva of *Simulium (Odagmia)* sp., a black fly (see p. 88-89)

Rat-tailed maggot: larva of **drone-fly** (see p. 69)

Larva of *Ptychoptera albimana*, a phantom crane-fly (see p. 77)

Tubifex sp., a sludge worm (see p. 170)

Erpobdella octoculata, a leech (see p. 166)

Bacterial plumes

These are only found in highly-polluted water. They are visible as coloured tufts, up to 150 cm long, attached to stones or plants, swaying in the current. They consist of a huge quantity of bacteria, sponges and unicellular creatures, especially ciliates. They convert both dissolved organic matter and small organic particles and thus help to purify a watercourse of organic substances. In highly nutrient-polluted water-courses you will often see filamentous algae, which can form entire 'ropes'. They can spring up very rapidly and can sometimes choke the entire water-course. Filamentous algae in large quantities can use up most of the oxygen in the water at night. They also shade out higher plants, which consequently disappear. In tranquil bays in slow-moving water there may also be large numbers of mosquito larvae (see p. 84-86).

Common fresh-water shrimp (see p. 126)

Larva of **Hydropsyche angustipennis**, a caddis fly (see p. 20-21)

Limnius volckmari, a riffle beetle (see p. 117)

Larva of **Sericostoma personatum**, a caddis fly (see p. 26)

Nymph of **Baetis rhodani**, a mayfly (see p. 54)

Nymph of **Blue-winged olive mayfly** (see p. 53)

River Lim-pet (see p. 155)

Nymph of **Isoperla sp.**, a stonefly (see p. 63)

Nymph of **Leuctra sp.**, a stonefly (see p. 64)

Glossary

Acidification is caused by sulphur, particularly in the form of sulphur dioxide, SO_2, which originates in such activities as the burning of coal and oil. Sulphur dioxide is a poisonous gas, which can combine with water in the atmosphere to form sulphuric acid. Acid rain can make freshwater acidic. Many animals are unable to tolerate acidic water, and acidified lakes tend to have reduced biodiversity.

Camouflage
In order to avoid being eaten by predators, many small animals have shapes and colours that resemble their surroundings. Case-building caddis fly larvae construct cases of stones, twigs, leaves etc. that resemble the bottom on which they crawl. Predators also camouflage themselves, the better to catch their prey. The Water Stick Insect, for example, resembles a thin plant stem, and leeches have colours that match their hiding places.

Cercariae are the third larval form of digenean flukes. They consist of a body with two suckers and a tail. They live pelagically, i.e. swimming free in the water, before boring into an intermediate or principal host. See flukes p.156.

Cold-blooded animals have a body temperature that roughly matches that of the surroundings.

Commensalism means that a species lives with another species without harming it, using it, for example, as a means of facilitating feeding, or as a means of transport from one place to another. Examples are non-biting midge larvae and Common Bithynia, or water mites and pond skaters.

Detritus is the accumulated dead remains of animals and plants. Detritus is an important food source for many water-dwelling invertebrates.

Diatoms are composed of only one cell, and have a chambered or pitted skeleton, shaped like two bowls. They can be round like a pill-box or elongated with a longitudinal furrow. They are usually brownish. Some live floating free in the water, while others cling to aquatic plants. Some are found in the mud on the bottom. See also p. 210.

Drift is a term for the phenomenon of animals being carried along watercourses by the current. In this way animals can spread to new areas downstream. Drift could empty the upper reaches of streams of small invertebrates, were it not for many adult insects flying upstream to lay their eggs. One example of this is the stonefly *Brachyptera risi* (p. 62). Animals that cannot fly, such as shrimps, make their way upstream along the banks or in eddies or in other sites out of the main current. Many small invertebrates in fast-flowing water are unable to avoid being occasionally swept away by the current and being carried some way downstream. This is countered by the fact that small animals in fast-flowing water often move against the current. This phenomenon is called positive *rheotaxis*.

Haemoglobin consists of an iron compound and a protein. Haemoglobin is found in the red blood cells of mammals, and can be found dissolved in the blood plasma of invertebrates. The iron compound takes oxygen from water or air, and the bloodstream conveys it round the animal's body. Here the oxygen is released where it is required, and the oxygen is replaced by carbon dioxide.

Imago is the Latin term for the adult insect.

Iridescent colours, seen primarily in insects, are due not to pigments in the animals, but to light of various wavelengths, reflected by sunlight and mixed together.

The **lake bed** in deep water has no plants, due to the lack of light. The top layer of water above is rich in microscopic plant plankton in summer and early autumn.

The **littoral zone** stretches from the water's edge to the limit of underwater rooted plant growth. Reed swamps may occur in this zone and the most diverse animal life tends to be found here.

Mining
Mines are tunnels gnawed in plant tissue by insect larvae. They do not break through the epidermis of the plant, and the mines are visible as pale areas in the tissues of the plant, particularly in the leaves.

Ochre pollution
In many areas, there is a large amount of iron in the ground. If the earth layers containing iron compounds lie beneath the water table, they are protected from oxygen in the air. But if the water table drops, due perhaps to excessive draining or pumping of groundwater, the iron may be oxidised, creating an iron compound that is easily dissolved and leached out. The water becomes red-brown.

If the leached-out iron compounds reach a stream, a further oxidisation occurs, and it is these oxidised iron compounds that are called ochre. They are visible as red-brown particles in the water and as layers on the bottom and on animals and plants. Water containing ochre can also be highly acidic.

Iron compounds are poisonous for many small animals and fish. They can also form a film on the gills of fish, and can block up the oxygen-providing organs of small invertebrates. Deposits of ochre on leaves can kill the plants. Ochre-tainted water also loses its clarity, hindering photosynthesis. Furthermore, it can ruin the spawn banks of salmon and trout.

There are very few bottom-dwelling animals in ochre-tainted watercourses. If the ochre is deposited as a layer on plants and stones, animals that feed on scraped-off algae will also fall in number. This applies particularly to snails and crustaceans. Most stonefly and mayfly nymphs disappear. Many caddis fly larvae and a large number of other water animals succumb, including shellfish that feed on microorganisms filtered from the water.

A few animals, however, can survive. This applies to the Alder Fly (p. 34), *Amphinemura standfussi*, a stonefly (p. 63) and *Prodiamesa olivacea*, a non-biting midge (p. 78), among others. Normally, though, a heavily ochre-tainted watercourse is a dead one, apart from a few varieties of bacteria.

Overwintering

Most small animals in ponds and lakes prepare for winter during the autumn, and as long as the water is not covered in ice, they have no problems. They are at a stage that is suitable for getting through the winter, as an egg, for example, or a larva/nymph or pupa. The few that can be seen are often sluggish with the cold.

Daphnia have mated, and the eggs now lie well protected in the mother's carapace, called the ephippium. Rotifers, moss animals and freshwater sponges also form overwintering stages, which are also suited to spreading the animals from place to place. Copepods, by contrast, continue their ordinary lives even in winter, and it is not uncommon to see them with egg sacs in icy water.

Most species of insect overwinter as larvae. Water bugs and water beetles, however, overwinter as adults. They could fly away in the autumn and overwinter on land, but they stay in water all through the winter, surrounded by air bubbles, although adults that have lived in small, shallow ponds with few plants during the summer look for larger ponds or lakes with plenty of plant life to provide oxygen even if there is a covering of ice.

The Water Spider overwinters in its bell or in an empty snail shell. The snail shell is filled with air and can be seen drifting on the surface or frozen into the ice.

Snails and leeches dig down into the bottom, as do a number of frogs. Other frogs and newts, however, crawl onto land and overwinter buried beneath tree roots, in mouldy tree stumps, under loose bark, under stones or in hollows in the ground.

Water is a more stable site than land for overwintering. Unless it is a small pond that can freeze solid, there will always be liquid water, i.e. water warmer than zero degrees. On land, the temperature can drop much lower, and in addition, there can be great variations in temperature. The only problem for the water animals is the ice covering the water. As long as the ice is clear, the plants can still produce oxygen by photosynthesis, but if the ice is covered in snow, no oxygen is produced, and if the snow cover is long lasting, the animals underneath may ultimately die from a lack of oxygen.

In hard winters, slow, shallow streams may freeze. This does not usually harm animal life, but in spring, when the ice breaks up, ice floes can be forced against the banks by the current, churning them up, and causing displacement of some animals, eggs and pupae.

On very cold, clear nights, ice may be formed on stones in shallow stretches of streams. If the ice layer is big enough, the stones can become so light that they are pulled away by the current and carried downstream. In this way the bottom can change in nature over a long stretch in just one night.

Papillae are wart-like protuberances.

Parasites live on or in another animal, feeding on it. The animal the parasite is living in or on is called the host.

Pelagic animals live free in the open water, either swimming or as plankton.

Physical gill
Some water-dwelling insects, e.g. water beetles, obtain oxygen from a mass of air held close to their bodies with water-repellent hairs. When the oxygen in the air mass has been used up, the insect must go up to the surface for a new supply of air.

A **plastron** is an extension of the physical gill, and is found for example in *Aphelocheirus aestivalis* (p. 92) and *Elmis aenea* (p. 117). An air mass is held tightly to the body by a dense layer of extremely fine hairs. The spiracles of the animal are in contact with the air mass, which acts as an external gill. New oxygen from the water gradually enters the air mass as the animal uses it, and carbon dioxide from the used air seeps out. This means that the animal does not need to come up to the surface to breathe.

A **puparium** is the name for the final skin of a fly larva. It stiffens as a firm capsule, like a pupal skin around the larva. Only when the adult insect is fully developed does the puparium burst open.

Spiracles are the openings on an insect's body through which it can take air into the branching network of air ducts known as tracheae.

Symbiosis
A relationship between two different species, in which both members benefit. An example is the Green Hydra (p. 173), which lives together with single-celled green algae.

Tentacles are longitudinal extensions from an animal. They can be smooth, like those of moss animals, or alternatively, they can be covered with cnidoblasts that can paralyse prey with poison, like those of freshwater polyps. Their function is to catch small invertebrates or particles in the water and transfer them to the animal's mouth.

Terminal hooks are protuberances on the caddis fly larva's rearmost segment. Each has a powerful claw.

Tracheae are the air ducts through which air is brought into the insect's body, to the organs where the oxygen is to be used.

Zooplankton are very small animals, such as water fleas and copepods, that drift free in open water, feeding on phytoplankton.

Further reading

C. Bronmark & L.-A. Hansson
The Biology of Lakes and Ponds
OUP 1998

M. Chinery
Collins Field Guide – Insects of Britain
and Northern Europe
Harper Collins 1993

R. Fitter & R. Manuel
Field Guide to Freshwater Life
Collins 1986
(out of print)

P. S. Giller & B. Malmqvist
The Biology of Streams and Rivers
OUP 1998

M. Guthrie
Animals of the Surface Film
Naturalists' Handbooks 12
Company of Biologists

Freshwater Biological Association Keys
Detailed keys to many groups

Index

Larvae and nymphs **x 1**

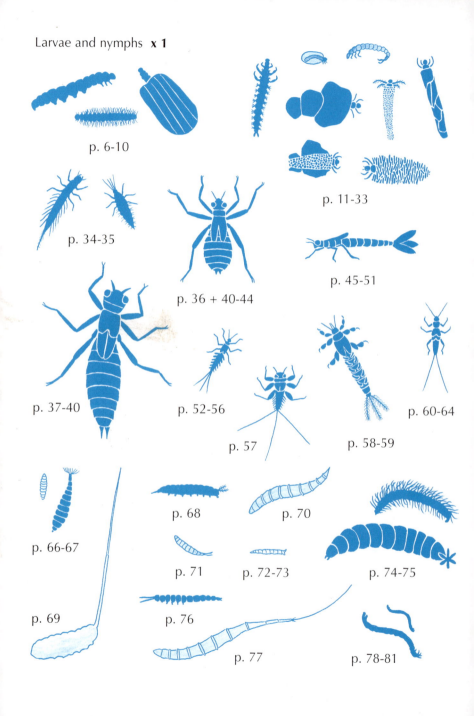

p. 6-10

p. 11-33

p. 34-35

p. 36 + 40-44

p. 45-51

p. 37-40

p. 52-56

p. 57

p. 58-59

p. 60-64

p. 66-67

p. 68

p. 70

p. 69

p. 71

p. 72-73

p. 74-75

p. 76

p. 77

p. 78-81